LETTING GO

LETTING GO:

AN ANTHOLOGY OF LOSS AND SURVIVAL

Edited by Hugh MacDonald

Black Moss Press
2005

National Library of Canada Cataloguing in Publication

Letting go : an anthology of loss and survival / edited by Hugh MacDonald.

Poems and short stories.
ISBN 0-88753-393-0

1. Loss (Psychology)—Literary collections. 2. Canadian poetry (English)—21st century. 3. Short stories, Canadian (English) 4. Canadian fiction (English)—21st century. I. MacDonald, Hugh, 1945-

PS8237.L58L48 2004   C810'.8'0353   C2004-901870-1

Cover photo by Marty Gervais
Designed by Karen Veryle Monck

Published by Black Moss Press at 2450 Byng Road, Windsor, Ontario N8W 3E8. Black Moss books are distributed in Canada and the U.S. by Firefly Books, Firefly Books Ltd., 66 Leek Crescent, Richmond Hill, ON Canada L4B 1H1. All orders should be directed there.

Black Moss would like to acknowledge the generous support to its publishing program from the Canada Council and the Ontario Arts Council for its publishing program.

ONTARIO ARTS COUNCIL
CONSEIL DES ARTS DE L'ONTARIO

Le Conseil des Arts | The Canada Council
du Canada | for the Arts

Contents

Preface

My mother died just before New Years in 1997. Her last five years had been an ever-slowing dance to death with Alzheimer's. I discovered then the horrible, unavoidable ravages that the disease brings to its victims and their families. I also learned that even the most painful of experiences has a positive side. Even after my mother no longer recognized me as her son, it was possible to become her friend and confidant. I discovered ways to love my mother in a manner never dreamed of before the disease. After Alzheimer's, all of Mom's previously impenetrable social fences came down, the restraints that had until then limited her ability to trust the yearnings of her heart were suddenly gone, and a family relationship that had become a difficult duty and an arduous responsibility turned into a joy-filled friendship. Eventually, of course, all of her systems shut down and she was unable to communicate, so it was with relief I said good bye to her. But I did so grateful for those last five years. My first book of poetry *Looking for Mother* (Black Moss Press, 1995) grew out of that experience.

It might have been memories of that book that prompted Donna Gervais to phone me early in 2003 with not only the idea for this book, but also a possible title. She said that she and her husband Marty (the publisher of Black Moss Press and this anthology) had been talking and they thought it might be a good idea to do a book about loss, and specifically an anthology about surviving loss. Such a book was important. People needed to know that they were not alone at those frightening moments of loss and they had to be assured that they would get through them. "Marty and I agree that you're the best one to edit a book like that. We'll call it *Letting Go.*"

What could I say? It was an excellent idea. Nothing I had ever written had elicited a response even close to *Looking for Mother.* More recently, in March of 2002 I'd lost my wonderful and energetic 92-year-old mother-in-law, a woman who'd danced until the week she went into the hospital for the last time. Loss has become a regular part of my life and will be so until its end. But with every loss, I have the potential to gain in love and compassion. And to watch as my family and friends and I grow more compassionately human. That's what *Letting Go* is about.

Hugh MacDonald

Kelley Aitkin

Skin of the Forest

In the heat of the Ecuadorian lowland rainforest the mind is soupy, forgetful, but the body is remembering itself, an animal responding to its environment. Cells call to cells, human skin covered in a sheen of sweat, meets the skin of the forest.

My guide is Gabriel, a Quichua man who has lived here all his life. I am less than ten years his junior, but for the duration of our relationship, two and a half days within this brown and green world, he treats me as an honoured daughter and I put my faith in him. We do not bushwhack, for this area of the forest is protected rather than pristine, not groomed but guarded after a fashion by trails. Piles of dung, armadillo holes, reptile, bird and mammal tracks, flowing columns of ants and termites can be found on these narrow byways, but their main purpose is to keep humans out of the way of the forest so that they will do the least harm.

On my first morning with Gabriel, the light pattering of rain suddenly intensifies. Though the thick canopy protects us from the worst of it, he harvests large palm fronds and binds them with vine to a sapling. We stand under our *runa hausi,* temporary shelter, and listen to the drumming of the rain on the surrounding vegetation. The spirit of the woods, Gabriel says, *sacha runao ama sanga,* is beating the roots of trees to scare us. Years ago, his father encountered a hoofed man deep in the bush.

"My father said hello, but the man was mute."

Language is palimpsest.

Sometimes, Gabriel continues, the spirit appears in the form of a stranger or friend, and this person blows on your hair—he bends my head toward his own—to bestow his special powers upon you. I feel the whistling column of air hit my scalp.

I am here to absorb an atmosphere, the setting of the last chapters of my novel-in-process. Deeper in the forest, there is a small group of hunter-gatherers who fell monkeys with blow darts and cook at night so that the smoke of their fires will not be detected. The Taegeri want no contact with outsiders. With each encroachment of the petroleum industry and the colonists that follow, this nomadic group moves deeper into the Amazon Basin. They have threatened to kill anyone who seeks them out. For now, through fear and inaccessibility, they have managed to maintain their way of life. Their continued survival, however, depends on the preservation of virgin jungle and access to a larger gene pool, in other words, they must find a way to import women of child-bearing age. This real-life drama is the stage for my tale of two Canadian sisters, one of whom has gone missing in Taegeri territory. I am drawn to write about a growing phenomenon in the west, that hunger for union with the wild which increases as those places—and the people in them—are diminished by our consumption and control.

I want to steep myself in this environment for research, the better to recreate its tangled humidity on the page. And yet, there will be—there always is—another layer to the trip. My journeys are an old and automatic response; when the going gets tough or even just confusing, I get on a plane.

In 1983, I spent a year on the Ecuadorian coast with a friend. We lived in a house-on-stilts without running water or electricity. It was an experience of the elemental and the extraordinary. I flew back to Canada at the end of that year, perhaps for no other reason than to use the return portion of my ticket, but I'd been bitten, literally and figuratively, by the tropics.

At the beginning of 1987, my father died of pancreatic cancer. A suburban businessman, hobby gardener and golfer, he was also a brooder and drinker. He had material success but could neither get at, nor relieve what troubled him—his was the generation that would not look over its shoulder. Like most of my siblings, I both loved and feared him. The air around him crackled. I echoed that volatility, and unconsciously responded to what he had, for lack of any other graspable option, suppressed. Illness softened him, but we had so little time.

Shortly after his death, I bolted, taking another trip south. My friend had left the coast for the mountains and now lived in a rural area outside of Quito. I moved into her house, but our relaxed rapport was gone. When the opportunity of working in a boutique aboard a Galapagos tourist ship presented itself, I took it, inadvertently signing on for 45 days in paradise. The shop was open when the tourists were on board, which left me free, during their twice daily visits to shore, to tag along.

After the first weeks I knew the guides' spiels by heart. Onshore, I'd wander off by myself, find a suitable contour on hardened whorls of *pahoehoe* lava and lie down to watch frigates and boobies wheel in a perpetually blue sky. Sometimes, I was subjected to the timid scrutiny of Sally Lightfoot crabs or the bolder poke and strut of mockingbirds. Depending on the island, I might study the indifferent profiles of marine iguanas, or listen to the floppy shifting of a sea lion harem. But always, eventually, I'd think of the father I'd so recently lost.

If it is awful to miss someone we knew and loved well, it is worse to miss the parent who was there and yet unreachable. All opportunities to mend our lifelong distance had passed. I lay on the smooth lava rock and gave in to bewildered pain, anger, and a childish hunger for what I would now never have. Time passed. I seemed to sense when I needed to return to the landing stage and the *pangas* ferrying passengers to the ship. Each time I was a little less eviscerated by regret, a little less empty than before.

Annually, Dad had tried his hand at rock gardens, favouring the bright blossoms of portulaca. This otherwise humble plant covers the slopes of *Plaza Sur.* The island rises out of a protected inlet, a tilted volcanic shelf that drops away to open sea. Once a week for seven weeks, I climbed its paths. Each time I stopped at the cliff edge to watch gulls vie with shearwaters and pelicans for flight paths in the air, their spiraling choreography a blend of mayhem and precision. I looked out at sparkling ocean and down at crashing waves. It had taken me a year to find this, a year since I watched my father's swollen legs shuffle through their last hours in a small overheated hospital room beside the 401. Here was vertigo and exhilaration, drama and reach, here was the place that said both, 'It's alright,' and 'Nothing can be done.' Swallow-tailed gulls will always wheel and dive.

In '99 there is a kidnapping in an oil-rich province of Ecuador. Other incidents follow. I postpone first one research trip, then another. Finally, by late summer of 2001, my novel insists on completion. I book a flight for October. In September, two planes crash into the World Trade Center and my fear, once so specific to travel in and out of the rainforest, leaps to include air travel, anywhere. Nevertheless, like thousands of others, I fly. In Quito, I put my money in my boots and get on a bus.

My trip from the capital to the rainforest is uneventful but it isn't until I'm settled at *Jatun Sacha,* 'Big Forest' and walking on the trail with Gabriel, that the insecurity I was carrying vanishes. I settle into his pace. Because of his presence I am fearless and feel a part of this place at the green core of the world.

In two days, Gabriel is more of an intimate to me than my father was in his lifetime. That our intimacy exists at all has to do with where we are, and that yearning without which I seem incapable of traveling. But I think it is also an evolution of that earlier loss: what the universe made plain to me, and loneliness verified, the gods of childhood are just humans after all. Since his death, I've learned to love my father separate from the role I needed him to play.

Now my yearning, made more urgent by the events of September 11, is for the fathering of land and forest, for something resolute and ongoing, if not the certainty of safety then at least the logic of Nature 'red in tooth and claw,' and green and brown, something broader and hopefully more time-less than terrorism. Deeper in the forest are a people fathered by the for-est and hanging on. Though sometimes pestered by planes, they know nothing of the instant deaths of thousands of New Yorkers, the slower deaths of thousands of Afghans through 'collateral damage,' displacement and starvation. In *Jatun Sacha* I am far from Taegeri territory, but close, I hope to what they have always known and continue to choose, a sense of the forest as home. Between this idea and my North American ineptitude in this environment, Gabriel is a temporary bridge.

We cross many bridges during the hours we spend together, most of them a single log embedded in either bank of a gully or riverbed. When Gabriel is certain of his own footing he reaches back to me and I step up. The log is usually about as big around as my leg, and always damp because though there may be sun above, it never quite penetrates the thick canopy. We face upriver or downstream, we move our feet in synchro-nized and steady increments, until with a final jump to the opposite bank, we release each other's hands.

"Graçias, Gabriel."

"De nada."

He will go one and a half days before he asks, "What is your name?"

Wonderful irony, that I—who am so engaged in words, tripping over my boots as I scribble in my notebook the Spanish and Quichua phrases for medicinal plants—am nameless, and not just to my guide, but also to the trees and creatures of the surrounding woods. When the little miracle hap-pens, late on the second day, I think it is this anonymity that brings me luck; if my name is superfluous, an expendable brick in my identity, then maybe the whole wall of identity—familial, cultural, defining—can and should come crashing down.

Towards the end of our longest hike, Gabriel and I come to one of the kings of the forest, an ancient ceiba tree. These rare giants have survived to spread roots more than 150 meters over the forest floor. An aging landlord, the ceiba supports many tenants: llianas, orchids, bromiliads, parasitic plants, mosses. Its upper branches are a lively tenement for birds, bats, primates and squirrels. Down at ground level, a *gallinaso* has laid her eggs in a hollow between two of the tree's buttressed roots.

Gabriel boosts me, using his thigh as a stepladder, so that I can snap a quick photo. After the flash comes the whirring sound of rewinding film. The dark bird hisses and sidles over to shield her eggs. I jump to the ground, sheepish at bothering her nest, relieved that the last picture has been taken.

Which of us first spies the large butterfly, motionless on a nearby leaf? Fawn-coloured and owl-eyed in repose, we catch a glimpse of purple luminescence as it circles us. It alights on a plant just off the trail. I step closer. Even Gabriel is peripheral now, having turned down the path. I extend my hand.

The butterfly climbs aboard.

It takes over twenty minutes to walk from there out to the highway. The whole time, my knuckles are a butterfly's palanquin. Though Gabriel has forgotten my name, he is certain about how much ground we cover. He says it several times, "800 meters? Yes, 800 at least."

Later that evening I climb to my cabaña via a stairway cut into earth. The other buildings are dark and quiet but the damp woods are alive with sound: zings, hoots, the bellow of a toucan. I open the notebook and take up my pen.

Like holding a snake—a butterfly grips!—a butterfly has muscles!—a butterfly yearns for salt the way the rest of us yearn for love. I carried that butterfly, big as a small bird, on my hand for over 800 meters. I crossed a log bridge and avoided overhanging vines. Deked around poisonous plants, walked softly, carried a big butterfly. Tortoise shell. Calico. Inside, velveteen pattern, a semaphoring purple-blue. Body the size of my baby finger. Magic. We'd left the forest and were walking along the dirt road to the Station. When it decided to go, it was fluttering in a spiral around us before I noticed the lack of tension on my fingers. It landed briefly on my rubber boot, then flew, one last time, into the field. Heading home.

By silent agreement, neither Gabriel nor I tell anyone at the Station. For a few days, he and I have been two human animals in the company of the woods, peering into the undergrowth; wading in rivers; tramping up inclines and crossing swampy declivities; spooked by flying bats—themselves spooked by us—in an abandoned cabin; examining the carcasses of tarantulas; swinging on vines; gathering many names and shedding the only one that doesn't matter. And in the middle of that, a visitation, Order: Lepidoptera, a flash of purple blue. Though I search in a butterfly compendium created specifically for Jatun Sacha, I cannot find the species. Spirit of the woods? What Gabriel's father saw will not, indeed, should not come so easily to me. Years earlier, on another trip to the rainforest, I watched small boys pee in the sand to attract a cloud of *Phoebis* butterflies and *Urania* moths. Urine and sweat, the body discharges salt and the butterflies sup. The magic is being here under the tutelage of a remarkable man and, for a short time, the time it takes to walk 800 meters on a winding trail, a part of the woods—a creature as nameless as I when I carried it—reaching out to touch me.

Every time we go into the woods we can forget and remember. When he blew on my head that first morning, Gabriel was ridding me, for a few days, at least, of that shell, the who-I-think-I-need-to-be, so that I could remember, in the best and original sense of the word, re-membering, as of an amputated limb.

We came from this once, and for a few years yet, we can catch a glimpse of what it is like to belong.

Segun Akinlolu

Another Part of Me

(for Awesu)

I shall cry for you, my friend
(After the pain comes the laughter)

Extinct, those days of pride,
With a haughty shoulder
Bearing all the pain of the earth
In a tense pouch—
Contain it, please, contain it.

Absorb it, please, absorb it.
Cushion it, please, cushion it.
My days are fragile now,
Reborn in a glassy frame,
Each little turbulence brings a rattle
A shake, some moisture.
My hot tears flow
Up my face, down my nose...
I have truly learnt to be a man,
My boils burst no longer belatedly.
Pouch of pain, I beseech you
Calm not, please, calm not
Touch me not, soothe me not...

I shall cry for you, my friend
(After the mourning comes the dancing)
Celebrate another part of me
Drowned in this mire of vain-hopefuls,
Another voice, silenced in bloom.
Your tubby flowers whisper to the winds,
"Death is sweet, was swift, scented"
Still I cry for you
For someone else now plays your part
And your pregnant smile
Haunts my dreams.

I shall cry, mourn, mingle
With the jostling crowd
And reach out to soothe heavy hearts.
After the tears comes the feasting,
Beyond the confusion, sudden realization...
Your striving was not in vain
I live to tell the tale
And spread your glowing smile!

Shari Andrews

No Feathered Shuffling

Icy fangs hang along the eaves
as the cat pads across the table
taking the time to stretch each leg,
each paw luxuriously
just inches from the woman's nose
the way her youngest son
marks dates on the calendar, draws up a budget
now that he is preparing to leave.

The washing machine performs
its lonely belly dance in the next room
and her thoughts
are layers of snow on the spruce,
the roof of the bird feeder
so that the yard barely breathes
when she takes in her hands this empty nest,
turns it over and over

to see what emptiness is made of:
brittle leaves, bits of twine, sharp twigs,
an upside-down hat
where there is no feathered shuffling,
no two-step that her mind can do,
no settling of her arms and legs
inside such prickly walls
surrounding the hollow left behind.

Lost to Her

The seemingly erratic way a bee flies,
bumbles really from blossom to blossom
without apparent territory,

but rather engrossed perhaps in the drone,
the song of its wings,
a blur in the breeze.

She wonders if bees know this as happiness,
the way he is lost to her at this moment,
knows she would have to bellow
to pull him from his reverie
of molding to his use
every flake of snow that falls in the yard.

She hears the engine rev.
as he puts it in reverse, then forward.
The blade of the plow he jerry-rigged
to the front of the pick-up
scoops and pushes the banks
into even rows on either side of the driveway.

She gazes at him through the window,
a figurine in a china cabinet,
until the light as it falls
fills her with liquid honey,
until it doesn't matter anymore
that it was this kingdom

and not her face he anticipated
as he pushed the blankets off and dressed.

Jacqueline Bell

Hush

The hair sheds pigment like a disguise
What's uncovered lies beneath
the colored world—closer to bone and stone,
but fine

your hair was soft as moths

Skin loses elasticity—
what's within pushes against thinning
membrane, bides its time
looks out with expanding eyes
encompasses the whole show
the wideness of it
mess and all the wildness
turning owl-like to see
every facet.

As the body slows
this kindles.

What has lain dormant
is shifting, begins to stir—
                    they cannot tell us

            you tiptoed out as if we were sleeping children
            not to startle, not to waken

Oh, the orangeness of an orange
tang of pine, the lift and sway

these are drifting out like boats
that slip their moorings
                    or maybe it's you—moving

            we should have seen it coming
            weight loss, rings sloughed off—

That day you lost your wedding band,
I found it, so pleased—one thing recovered, held

onto and now it's mine—on this Mother's Day,
your loss springs out with
                    tulips, foreshadowing lilac.

Roger Bell

Burying Mel Hackett

Today I walk among the dead
I leave behind the springtime grave
where another part of me is freshly laid
and resolutely stride
up the bright hill of noon

past the man who owned the Five and Dime
and conversed with himself as if he alone
were the only one worth talking to
and past the one who ran the hardware store
where stovepipes mingled with bolts and paint

past the avid butcher who lopped off his fingers
past the librarian, she let me read until I was full
past the jolly fat man who dieted with cancer
past the dry grocer who sold sugar in brown bags tied with string
that he looped like legends from a roll in the ceiling
past the garage guy who dispensed three-decker cones
with greasy hands for a nickel a scoop, and chomped his cigar
past my father's mother
where she lies in the shade of a century maple
past the man who often took me swimming
and drowned by himself when the lake turned fickle

past the woman who soaped my mouth for swearing
past the gentle farmer who died dancing
past the head of the choir so proud of her singing

past my maternal grandparents, nearly thirty years gone
their sunny kitchen with the canary in the window
and the stew bubbling on the stove
alongside them their son taken too young
and his troubled son who hated the waking world
and now untroubled sleeps.

Today I walk among these welcome dead, past all this present past
to my parents who wait beneath the rain-loved turf
beneath their warm black polished naming stone
for their boy's first visit in all these long months
since August last lay ripe upon this peaceful park.

Sonnet upon your parents' passing

- for Carolyn

The wind has stiffened, now to the north-northwest
and those last stubborn leaves, dyed deeper brown
with age, have been subdued, are all but down
where, slumped in drifted dreams, they've joined the rest.

There's early morning woodsmoke sharply spun
mingling with the wake of geese, their farewell cries
over the muted lake, along the newborn ice
upon thin air, among the strands of sun.

They were just here, it seems, and now they're not
and everywhere you look the season's turned
too soon, although you wish it back, although you yearn
your pleas seem numb, the day dumb with regret.

Then like the sign you hunger for so much
upon your upturned face, the snow, a reassuring touch.

Marianne Bluger

The Silence After (a tanka sequence)

singing somewhere
in this unraveling mist
a thrush
but Dad today
no longer in this world

*

banging
banging
like a fist in rage
his old shed door
as we sort Dad's things
*

what to do
with these stacks of his prized
mathematical journals
I never even
attempted calculus
*

is it somewhere here
my destiny – among the jumbled oddments
in his dresser drawer
on this creased Nazi paper
stamped with a yellow star
*

where last fall
he limped along by my side
in a clutch
of damp lilac
I bury my face
*

still
by the pond – empty
beaded with rain
the iron bench
where we stopped to rest
*

from an orphan
dream of lostness
I waken
to hear night rain
elaborate the silence
*

in the bitter cold
my useless tears
making
the blue stars
twinkle

     *

steaming up the windows
on the stove it simmers
smelling delicious
I have followed exactly
Dad's recipe for borscht

     *

he left me
these blue hyacinths
he loved
it's April night forever
my Dad's birthday

     *

swaying
in my hammock
as birches
catch the last light
I think of my folks

     *

when these birches
were planted my Father
was living
my Auntie too – I remember
them laughing together

coda

above my desk
the photo of a haggard
Berlin Jewish youth
is watching me
write you this

Nollaig Bonar

A Sense of Women Gone

Afire with sickly, thickly head
and shallowed gasps
so's not to stir my raw-chopped gullet,
clamping my pillow I clump
the hall in darkened time in search
of rest in the cooler spare room bed.
And stretching my legs under the cover
I bury myself up to the nose to save
the icy air for breath alone.

And a scented wisp curls up and into me
and stirs my friend in me.
Patchouli oil—her scent of choice.
And though ten months and many
guests and launderings have passed since
she slept here
still the scent of her wafts up
and brings her close.

                    *   *   *

Leather-brown gloves clumped in a ball
that feels like oily, stiffened
seaweed thrashed up on shore,
are in my winter pocket.
Bought one Christmas for my mother
who swore
it was iced water and not blood at all
that ran through her veins.

Always and ever cold.

And when they cleared out her things
two years and more ago,
they returned this once-gift.
Now I wear the leathers that covered
her ice-cold hands.

And on the year's first cold day,
I rummage in winter pockets
in search of that clod of leathery brown.
And writhing, stretch my fingers to make way and shape
in through her gloves.

And then it comes—
the scent,
the wispy waft of her, from deep
within the palm's interior—
a handful of that fancy perfume smell,
so known from her handbag,
her wallet opened for pennies for Black Babies,
even the roll of mints, to stop the tickle in her throat
took up the scent of perfume,
and with the scent comes a flash of spittled hanky
yanked across my dirty face in the back seat.

*　*　*

And in my sickly, sorrowful state I pine
for lost girlhood when I could clamber
into the warm spot
of the beds of one, the girl
the other, mother
and snuggle the length behind them,
breathe in their scents,
and by hum and drone of their voices
find restful sleep.

Profound Loss of Hearing

She had no problem with her hearing,
her loss of hearing was
little loss to her,
not as long as her eyes held out;

She took to mouth gazing and figuring
words from mouths' shapes.

No loss to her but great to others;
so for their peace and
sakes she got a hearing aid and was
　　　　barraged by sound all round no back no middle ground
　　　　sound just noise aclamour barging and assaulting her.

For her peace and sake she gave it up and suffered
their impatience at not being heard.

Much later then a new device a tiny
shell implanted—
wire and double A battery—
so simple,
it brought her sound in single mouthfuls
and changed her life
profound she said
when she heard again the sound of birds.

Widowed Words

The new-made widow man draws close
to her who made him so,
and bending low, sounds words in mother
tongue—word sense and sound
of love and grace.

No child of his recalls such words from him
except perhaps on way back school nights
translating Irish homework.

Virginia Boudreau

Around the Mulberry Bush

Those last days, dad, when
you lay disconnected
insidious
moles of brown velvet
broke surface on
your face, your shrunken
hands to herald lost
moments when nothing
rhymed

your eyes
fog shrouded ellipses of sea
closed with the effort
of trying and i watched the colour
fade in fruitless searching

when the words stopped funneling
in a vortex to nowhere
and your mouth
finally opened a black well
for your very essence to seep through

i liked to imagine your thoughts
swirling joyful in pink
clouds of cherry petals
snowing over cherished
nooks in grandma's yard
each spring a haze
of children with silvered
voices unfurling banners of laughter

to rise above the wind

Treasures

Lupins rise
in a lavender cloud
misting the hill.

yellow finch lilts
fresh as the breeze
bending birches.

On days like this
when the sadness
is a well

I'll reach out
with both hands
and grasp.

I'll covet
these treasures
that Earth offers up

with a heart
that has not yet learned
to withhold.

Private Drive

Come early summer, drilled tin discs
shimmered in the two cherry trees
beside the woodpile
their tinging on the wind
warded off crows
my grandfather always said
but, they made me think of
Christmas

Grandma, in her flowered housedress
lilac, misty blue pegging
a row of gingham dishtowels to

sway on the frayed rope line
through sultry afternoons
over hedges of wild mallow,
the hum of honeybees

Scotch pines dropped
coral needles, rice paper cones
on worn path to "the point" a single
twisted apple tree bearing hard
sour fruit, the glitter of the lake
on all sides where a boy
had drowned years before
my mother's voice following

Then, the cove was our oyster
painted wood rowboat cradled in
lily pads, turtles slipping from
fallen logs as we pulled on splintered oars
water drops glinting in the sun
pooling perfect Os on the pond

View of the river beyond the porch
bridge in the distance, spanning sleek
speckled flow a canoe gliding
silent through the mist, the eddies
and once a moose waded out through
silvered stalks of bulrush, offering seed
to autumn wind

The oak corner cupboard darkened and filled
cottage crockery, daffodils, jonquils
green fluted rims, richness of cream
their clatter on the heavy table
the sound of laughter, sweetness of blueberries

Barn swallows swooping in verandah eaves
the croak of bullfrogs, breaking still dusk
fireflies hovering, igniting spikes of broom
moon splaying ochre fan on black lake

Ours, for remembering.

Laurie Brinklow

Hope Chest

My mother's hope chest always sat at the foot of my parent's bed.
When I was twelve I learned how to open it: silken blond veneer
concealed a red cedar heart. Ran hands over wood, closed my eyes,
breathed Vancouver Island green.

There I found a compartment of a mother's life: blue baby sweater,
first pair of shoes, Yogi Bear piggy bank, a boxful of sympathy cards,
newspaper clippings and an obituary for a green-eyed child. *Greggy
drowned in a bathtub, Greggy drowned in a glass of water.*

Greggy was playing too close to the edge one spring and fell into the
creek dressed in his snowsuit. The newspaper said the current carried
him six miles in two hours before he was finally stopped. *Greggy
drowned in the bathtub, Greggy drowned in a glass of water.*

He was two and I was five, and my parents were eight hundred miles
south and I remember they flew home right away but not fast enough
to save us.

My mother lives in an apartment now. Her hope chest sits beside
my bed. My daughter asks, *What's in there, Mom?* Blankets, I tell her,
just blankets.

Prince George

A trailer park on the other side of the tracks where boys impatient to
get anywhere dare each other to roll under the trains between
shudders of coupling and uncoupling, learning young that timing is
everything.

Two miles from school to home, kicking the same rock to make the
walk go faster, and there's Uncle Mike with my dad at the kitchen
table full of beer bottles and ashtrays, their shadows shrouded in
smoke. Not really our uncle but we've called him that since we were

little in Dawson Creek, where we used to live. He's hauling the mail from Vancouver, decided to break his trip halfway. We make ourselves scarce, to our homework and library books, stray strands of voices and the stink of stale beer seep under our doors.

Bedtime and they're still at it, Seagram's now and they're getting blurry, tongues fat as Mrs. Bushby's dachshund in the trailer across the road, and through the walls laughter careens, ice cracks, liquid swishes as more rye is poured.

Then quiet, scary quiet. Something I've never heard before. The sound of a man crying.

How can he ever forgive himself, or Aunt Annika, for trusting a two-and-a-half-year-old to stay away from the spring creek at the end of the road, or his kids for running home, singing *Greggy's gone swimming, Greggy's gone swimming,* or his own kids for living.

Greggy, the child who ate a whole package of chocolate ex-lax, the child who fell into the septic tank, the child who'd look you in the eye as he'd pick up your mother's favourite green glass ashtray and drop it, laughing. Greggy the magic child, Greggy the push-the-limits child, see Auntie Annika running frantic, *this can't be happening, if I just close my eyes and open them again he'll be there, laughing, laughing.*

Uncle Mike stops crying, I hear the front door close, his truck shatter stillness. I don't hear my father go to bed. In the morning, all the ashtrays full, the bottles empty.

Ronnie R. Brown

Visitation

Perhaps it was the pain-killers
scrambling her brain, or maybe
it was a dream. She knows
that they are
the most logical

explanations why
on the night after her baby came
too soon, the night after she'd laboured
for nothing, knowing that she must push,
push, like the doctor
said, knowing
that the child
she was urging out
was unready
to be born
her grandmother appeared
at the foot of her hospital bed
with a pink-blanketed form cradled
in her arms whispering, *don't worry, darlin'*
I'll care for her until
you can be here. Whispering,
don't you worry none, sweetheart,
you won't have to come for years and years yet, but
when you do this moment will seem
like yesterday, like none of us have ever
been apart. Then she blew a kiss
and disappeared. Her grandmother,
eight years dead, standing
in the sterile white room
offering love, comfort
the promise
of eternity.

Final Photographs

She is ironing
passing the tefloned metal
over clothes
too long in the plastic basket
pleased at how the gusts of steam
are able to overcome
even weeks, months of neglect.

In the basement,
the closest phone
a floor away, she feels
safe. The kids will never
wander down. They know
what will happen, at best
a lecture on responsibility,
at worst
the aging Procter-Silex
passed to them, followed by
their mother
marching defiantly
up the stairs.

Sometimes she hopes for this,
a chance to "teach them
a lesson," but today
she's glad to be ironing,
alone—the private satisfaction
of making things smooth
with just a pass
of the hand.

While she irons,
her husband   flies
far from their basement
he is passing
over borders, provinces, states
to the bed where his only brother lies,
dying. Soon his plane
will set down, be exchanged
for a rented car. Soon...

But for now
while he flies,
while blood oozes from his brother's
body (a haemorrhage
that won't be stopped. A dying
that is already
inevitable) she irons.

In the basement she cannot see,
needs not think of these photos
framed and arranged beside others—
the children, her parents, their wedding—
gathering dust on the dining room hutch:

Her brother-
in-law at twelve holding
her three-year-old husband
on his knee. The two of them
brushing opposite borders
of the family grouping
at their parents' fiftieth
anniversary. The brothers, book-
ending their almost ninety-year-old father.

"I want to take this now,"
she can still hear her
sister-in-law insisting
as she positioned the three of them,
"who knows when you'll be
together
again."

Soon
her sister-in-law
will repeat those words
as she takes snapshots
of friends, family
during the small reception
that will follow
the funeral. All too soon
father and son will be together
again, leaving her husband
behind, the last one standing
on this side
of eternity.

The iron hisses
as she glides it across
a wrinkled shirt arm
moving back and forth, back
and forth until
it looks perfect,
like new. Mechanically
she retrieves another
starts the process
over again, glad
that there is so much
to be done,
so much here
that she can do.

Dream Camera

Hasn't she read
of something like this.
a camera
that photographs
dreams? Science
fiction probably,
but who knows?
People rocket
through space, golf
on the moon.

She doesn't dare ask, but
if a camera like that exists
she wants it.

Then, at last,
she would have proof
of the way her father
smiles at her in dreams. Stills
of his face softening as he tells her
he's sorry for everything,

really does love her, has
all along.

Glossy finish
or matte, all she wants
is a few small rectangles
she can slip
into the family album
to help refocus
her memories,
just a few prints
of the images
that have been developing
in her mind
forever.

Margo Button

Still-Lives

For Randall, 1967-1994

—What is a man...who has no landscape? Nothing but mirrors and tides.
Anne Michaels

Suddenly an old man,
you approach me in a rocking chair
though I don't understand how.
I squeeze in beside you but you draw away.
Supplicant, I lay my face against yours.
Please, for a minute, my son.
Eight years since I felt your warm young skin
against mine, that wiry hair.
What a good view from my chair, you say,
quite at home with being dead.

I want you to know I didn't die of a broken heart
the way mothers are supposed to.
Days go by when I never think of you.
Don't blame me. When you turned your back
I went looking for a dream at the end of the world
where nothing reminds me of you.
New friends for family. A garden
where the parson-bird sings
his long-winded song in the kowhai tree
and the euphorbia hangs over the flooded brook
like a drama waiting to happen.

We Were Going to the Orphanage

—for Randall 1967-1994

We were going to the orphanage
on embassy business. So maybe,
we told our son — floating the idea —
we might find a little girl
looking for a family.

When she didn't appear at dinner
he started to cry. Yes,
he wanted a sister. Oh yes.

Our strapping twelve-year-old,
the karate wannabe
who waited behind the door
and leapt out at us
like Tarzan on a gazunga.

RANDALL, I'd scream. RANDALL,
the parrot shrieked.
(loud but not loud enough
to wake the dead).

I'd start laughing
and the parrot would mimic me

so I laughed even more
and we'd all crack up.
That house was bedlam.

Then Andrea moved in
trailing giggles
like bubbles behind her
and Randall wanted to send her back.

To Learn Non-Attachment

1

Spend two years
in a Tibetan monastery.
Make the same mandala
day after day
until you learn it by heart
according to the exact proportions
laid down in ancient texts.
Meditate on love
while you rub the horn
on the ridges of the chukpa and
watch the multi-coloured sand
trickle into an intricate design.
When the mandala is finished
destroy it,
gather up the grains,
pour them into the sea.

Start again.

2

Give birth to a son.
Teach him wisdom,
cloak him with love.
When he dies
after twenty-six years
scatter his ashes in the sea.

Goodbye Alina

wearing the necklace
i made you out of

the strong
bits of my broken

heart the subway splits
your image into

squares of light as if
you are already

beginning to vanish
into that other

country of solid
winters, where

sleep is the
sediment on the bottom

of a bottle
of wine and oh,

i hope
for more for you: that forest

with its cabin
and the silver trees

where you snapped
photos of firewood, enveloped

contrast for the
first time, closed

the shutter
on the summer

of the unconditional
and took what you could

keep - the clearest
edges, those ribs of light

Greg Cook

Dear Mother

i

Dear Mother, this poem began
as a letter to father
another since my last to him
twenty years ago
though he was then forty years
dead and buried over seas
always salt within us

The first thing I planned to say
was how you have him
fighting more battles
now landing at Normandy
that memorial day
though he was still in Canada
impatient for the thick of it

Your putting him over early
is no loss of memory
Your reliving of battles
as though they won the war
before he got there
is the best invention
We are born to rebuild

ii

I know your telegram
was routed to your father
who brought you confirmation
that my father was killed
an official scrap of paper
of his last breath an ocean away

I also realize
the flock of birds at the lilac
were not arriving on their shadows
outside the kitchen window
that mourning of long listening
They were leaving like so many dreams
away from your inhaling your screams

Perhaps your stoking the fire
let a stove cover ring
feathers wing between lilac leaves
– ten days before his body
was brought in from the flooded field
– the morning you climbed the wood pile
and fell to the sound of his voice

iii

I wanted to tell him
how you place your wreath
under his name embossed in brass
on the town cenotaph
how you will take it next Sunday
to his cemetery marker
in his ancestor's plot

Meanwhile how
the afternoon of Remembrance
you hold his buddy's wedding gift
– a studio portrait:
he in his army cap
smiling in your lap
growing younger each year

Carlinda D'Alimonte

Abiding Mama

The day mama
died
was

like tasting the words on the last page
of a novel I did not want to put down,
like a soft fade to black after being lost
in a movie that's come to an end,
like house lights exposing the real picture,
like at last turning
a corner inside the cage
and finding the door open,
like having no bills to pay
like having one thing to do,
like an end to ramming
myself against a rock wall
and instead relaxing on its warm surface

The day mama died
was

like dissolving
the jagged edges of my life
leaving me ready for play,
like December wind
on a June day
or fog descending
like wearing a single yoke
and releasing half my cargo
like letting the sun set
like burying the albatross
like, at last, drowning small pests,
and passing explosives
to the next player

like heaven opened up, permanently

The day mama died was
letting go of a thing
I'd been torturing
between thumb and finger

laying down my weapons,
surviving a catastrophe
dead silence
                    after thunder

the day mama died was like kneeling alone before the sky

Julie Denison

A Call to Prayer

> ** Amrit Vela: 3 to 6 AM, the hrs. considered most amenable to
> meditation.*

It's three AM and,
choking on the morning ritual
          of too-green wood
          smoke wafting up the back stairs,
                    Shelagh mutters, ". . . *Reg?*"
                    (that's "rage," not "Reg"—
she is an Aussie)
as she scratches for the
          puckered absence of a breast.

          As kettles clang beneath her,
                    newpaper is torn and rattled.
                    Shelagh's too-thin fingers'
shock at downy sensitivity
instead of hair upon her head, and nausea,
          is routine as running water now—

and Reg's heavy feet. The thud of
                    wet birch thrown into the Franklin stove
                    asks Shelagh if she will consume or be
consumed: a simple glass of water,
pills, pills, pills.

          Is it her adamantine will,
          or just the fragrance of
                    darjeeling in the dark that coaxes her
                    to every morning swear
she will outlive the threadbare
crimson of that robe he brought
          back from the Punjab years ago;
          that in the startled face of death,
                    she will, despite the chemo and the bathos,
                    blast her optical prosthesis—
blast the sun, moon, stars and all
the other weary lights of *Amrit Vela*—
          into darkness with . . .
          if not a smile, then dignity.
                    Her will is all one thought,
                    one blazing single eye.

Yvette Doucette

Relationship

We wade in the known: this dark brown eye, that funny toe,
these repetitive emotions, our stories handed down.

For my mother
now
the unknown lies just there
          her pulse beating wildly in her wrist,
every bone rendered exquisitely visible,
her ears perfect cowries, conch, abalone.

My hands run over buckled spine, her skeletal hips,
the sudden knowledge of the nearness
giddies me.
We are so close
to the other places
a few heartbeats away—

We are alive, we breathe
and all
lies between us,
shadowy and real;
the happy voices heard in dreams, the telephone calls that come just when
they are needed, the pain we share,
all the moments that make us, bind us.

We die. We leave behind the shell, to dust.
We die. We wander in the open place,
never far,
just there.
My mother turns her face to the window.
The elm branches are bare,
the skies low and scudding with November's afternoon light,
the clouds parting, concealing, strung together with subtle edges.

Thoughts of snow
hang between us.
How she found it glorious, mysterious
walked for hours listening to the chickadees
among the sugar maples.

Her pale tea skin has bleached forty seasons from the equator.
Away from Jamaica's frangipani and hibiscus, fat and luscious aloe,
the bright and riotous—the nourishing and healing.
Here on Prince Edward Island,
green
acre upon acre of apple green,
thick clover green, delicate timothy, spruce and fir green,
the verdant grace won her ample heart.

Autumn
gives way to early winter's browns and grays, and frozen red clay muck—

　　　　　　my mother's eyes and mine cast toward the ground
they lift up as one pair
unexpectedly
joyful

the chilling air filled with white, the tree line, the fading light—
perfect snow moving across the field, blown by a northeast wind.

Jannie Edwards

What to Do When You Lose a Daughter

Make a willow hut from your grief.

1.
When the ground thaws deep enough,
dig a trench in a circle
wide enough to lie down in.
Dig it to your knees.

This will be the hardest part.
You will want to throw yourself down.

But you will keep on digging
through the black wound of your rage
through the raw wound of your love.

You will keep on digging
until the only voice that makes sense
is the mantra of your muscles
growing hard under your toughening skin.

One day, the trench will be finished.
But you have just begun.
Until snow completely fills the trench,
feed the earth with scraps from your kitchen—
That way, you will be reminded to eat.

Remember how when she was a seed
growing in your private sea,
your law was to give, hers to take
Remember how you obeyed.

The first winter will be long and dark.
You will turn your face to the wall.

2.
When the days begin to breathe again,
and ice starts to break up,
go in the early morning to a river you know well
Sit by the river.
Listen
as it begins to wake up—
ice creaking and banging,
sounds of running water.

Remember how you watched her sleeping.
When her eyes opened, without surprise,
she looked right into your eyes
without alarm, like an old soul.
As if she knew it would be you
and you would be waiting.

Just before the sun sets
when you can feel frost forming a skin,
this is when you must cut your willow branches.

Pick the branches that look dead.

3.
Plant the sticks in the trench
a hand-width apart, your fingers stretched
as far as they will go.
Water the sticks every day.
Watch the sky for rain.

Wait.

You will feel invaded by weariness.
You will feel old as stone.

4.
One day, you will see the first buds.
Perhaps there will be a storm brewing,
thunder on the move.
Perhaps you will hear your first robin.
You must be patient.
Sometimes, snow can come in May.

5.
In a few years,
faster than you think,
the trees will be saplings.
Their supple grace will break your heart.

In the spring just as they are budding,
now you must begin to weave them.

Plait the branches as you gathered her hair
into a thick braid that day by the sea
when she got her first woman's blood,
and you swam together until you felt cleaner
than you'd ever felt before.

Tie the woven branches into a dome.

6.
You will be amazed how quickly willow grows.
In a few more years, the thickened trunks
will close the hand spaces of your planting.
In the full leaf of summer,
you will not be able to see sky
through the green roof.
Willow suckers will crisscross the floor.
Children will want to play there,
share cool secrets.
You will not mind if they do.

You will prefer to lie down in the hut
in early spring,
late fall, the hinges of your hips creaking.

Most of all in deep winter,
when the silver ribs of the roof
pattern the cold, dark bowl of sky
spilling over with stars.
You move your arms and legs slowly:

up and down
apart   together

A snow angel

This is what you have been waiting for.
This mute push toward light,
this dark reaching.

Mark Featherstone

Starling

I found a starling in the basement
behind the furnace.
When I tried to lift it, all its feathers
slumped from a parched
and empty skeleton.

No trumpet answers this creature's dying,
the last selah of its three-chambered heart.
The sea-change passes unremarked,
stirs no bell from slumber.
No walls drip blood,
no attic moans,
no light blinds the brain.
Departing life disturbs
no surface as it goes.

Even for those I love the most,
no mystic signal will interrupt
no quotidian diversions, distract

me from the lawn mower's track, from cracking
ice upon my windshield, from filling
out my taxes.

Nothing like that story of a mother wrenched
from sleep by a dreamt-of son at the very
moment, as it turns out, his lips go cold
against the mud of no-man's land
between two trenches.

Isn't this why we read once more the plays,
listen to the actors time and again
repeat their solemn lines to a dram of poison,
a happy dagger? We watch them die over
and over so that (though the shade glides past
unnoticed) we can say, I was there.
I saw it all. I heard everything.

You, Alfred Wegener

The child tucks one foot behind a knee.
His right hand clasps an ear.
His left nestles in his sleeping neck,
remembering his geography.

I dreamt of continental drift
in Miss McGrath's grade two class.
I propped my cheek upon my fist
and heard the world map whisper

how the lap of the Caribbean
once held Saharan headland,
and how Brazil had warmed a shoulder
in the hollow of the Ivory Coast.

By the age of seven, you get the gist
that bodies—however well
they fit—will drift
apart, moving with a continent's

determination, divided
by resolute seas.

He turns from me, but snuggles closer.
His elbow finds his hip.
I lay an arm across and tease
my smallest finger
in his wakening grip.

Those still with Us

So like the dead to ring the bell and run
sniggering from the bushes

slipping into the house
before the front door closes

smoothing their lapels
in the backs of closets

sipping from our wine glasses
at family dinners.

They crowd us on the sofa
and laugh at their own jokes.

When the conversation lulls
they can't resist a time-worn yarn.

They point reproachfully
at their old chairs

sniff at the recipes
they taught us

even trick our vocal chords
with their own inflections.

They will not forsake us
we who shoulder their flesh and blood.

In their mercy
they will not make it

easy.

Pam Galloway

Traces

You are gone
from me, from our home.
Eager to claim my space, my time,
I gather up the bits you left behind. Shoes
eased off, one foot against the heel of the other
when you sat reading, too long, too late; your book
opened and turned face down; the mail
you had no time to open; on the balcony, your ashtray
piled high, dog-ends disintegrating in the rain (a rot
I stop my mind from contemplating).

Picking up, finding a place for things
tumbling from my overfull hands.
This is how my mother went round each room
after our visit, looking for books, toys,
jewelry we'd tossed aside then forgotten.
This is how mothers and fathers find
and hold onto the small, once insignificant,
treasures of a lost child; how bereaved
sons and daughters sift through
the layers of letters, cards, flowered and glittered
for every occasion, photos
that never made the albums, yellowed
recipes clipped years ago from the Woman's Page.
Death brings its demand for mementos.
In France, one summer, I came across a box

of a cemetery. A walled-in cube, stone tombs
built so close, impossible to walk between them.
And scattered over every surface:
framed pictures, rosaries, small bouquets,
fragments of life.

You are coming back,
sometimes I say, too soon. Let me keep
your books on the shelves,
your clothes in the drawers.
Good to be alone.
At night, I sit on the edge of our bed,
slip my arms into the sleeves
of your shirt, each small button's fastening
a painstaking measure of time.

Unexpected Gardens

—(in memory of Daniel)

Years since these stripped trees crashed on this beach.
They lie eased into rocks, water and wind softened
their bark cracked, rotted into unexpected gardens.
Grass and bramble thrive in knot-holes of decay.

Plants do this. Fireweed bursts from scorched ground
and full-grown trees are rooted in sheer rock.
In the midst of death: life, pushing
slight but persistent shoots toward light.

In the grain

(In memory of Bill Fairley)

At first you watched, stood beside him
all those chilly Saturday mornings,
followed his thick yet precise hands

stroking a fine length of fir.
Timber he called it, suggesting music
caught in the grain.

He taught you how to ease out wood's tone,
set of the saw, the start of a cut
and how to stay straight, keep time
with his steady back and forth.
His solid grip guiding your hand.

You held the tools: mortise-gauge,
set-square, bradawl and bit.
Their names, lyrics he never forgot.
You turned their weight,
tipped a spirit-level to find true.

Now, when you lean into the plane's glide
or turn a paintbrush to cut in clean,
he's there; humming the first line
over and over. Both of you
lost in the build.

Kathlene Hamilton

Clapiston Corner

My father is forever young
and I am forever abandoned.

I remember his face framed in gold
on my mother's bedside table
So handsome was he in our pretty company
A beautiful male ghost
in the feminine apartment of "Carol and the girls"

I was the oldest of the girls and I knew he was dead.
Knew about the car accident
was bold enough to ask my mother how he'd gotten

from the highway pavement to heaven
She said the angels flew down and got him.

My father is my phantom heart
I feel sometimes as though I still have one
and then I remember
he's dead.

My father is forever 17
immortalized in black and white
framed in gold
and his eyes are sad
as though he knew his tragedy.

As though he knew he'd leave me forever
and all I'd know of him was his old broken-stringed guitar
that I pulled out of my bedroom closet to play
on days when my mom hit me with the wooden spoon.

My father loved cars
was fixing one up for me, his first born,
so he must have loved me.
When I was three years old and
he drove his car into the
back of a transport truck
near Clapiston Corner on his way
home from Hamilton,
he must have loved me.
Even though I'm told
perhaps he drove into that truck on purpose,
perhaps he killed himself on purpose, he still
could have loved me.
He would not have known that when
I was five years old, I'd race to a knock
at the door to see a woman standing there, wearing
a smart little suit and carrying a smart little briefcase and
that she'd ask, "Is the man of the house home?" And my mother
would move in behind me and say, "I'm a widow" and the woman's
smile would drop and her voice lower in pity and I'd shut the door in
shame as she said, "I'm sorry".

I would forget all about him for days at a time—until
I'd run with my little sister to the lobby on the first floor, to
all those neat little silver boxes and before I inserted the key
 to collect my mother's mail, I'd read the label
"Mrs. Robert Vance"
and I'd remember.

And more days would go by, hot summer days when
I'd explore new neighborhoods on my blue bike and pick
wild cucumbers from the empty lot across the street, and
wait for the train out back so I could run in front of it without
getting hit and I'd never think of him until Tracy and Joanne Ireland started
bragging about how when their dad got home from working at the fire station,
because *"our* Dad is a fireman" he was going to take them to the Dairy Queen for
ice cream cones. And I'd say something about my mom or my uncle or somebody
and they'd think I missed the point so they'd say, "You don't even have a Dad."
I remembered him then. When I knew I was too dirty and bad to deserve a father.

And then a man came and slept in my mother's bed and my father's photograph
disappeared.

gillian harding-russell

a smell of leaves

in advance, I see the mess of plates
(the reason obscurest
when we have broken
this food), kids out

the door, dog escaped
greeting a neighbour, flying lick of love
hurled at a stranger stopping to pet her

(here I am left meticulous
and ridiculous, Queen of Pentacles
in the company of dirty plates)

From the kitchen window, I hear
a dog bark (not ours thankfully,
crouching like second nature
at my feet, but expectant)

Out the window
incessant fire of yellow leaves

I must walk the poor dog.

A conference of geese, decisions,
smell of leaves, smoke, dampness
rising in the evening
cool

a curl of wind, whiff
of fear, distrust, something
maybe worse

than this fatigue—

"Take us to the park, Mummy—."

We are dirt

We threw her ashes
into the white, white whorl of one gigantic wave
a tongue rolling, unwinding
the long shore   Open mouth

where oceanic sands retract
ripple waves
on the roof of the world

the floor of the widening
sky   opals
refracting colour
in light

conch and periwinkle, upturned
listening with a million ears

invisible rainbow of D.N.A.
distinguishing grain
from grain—

indistinguishable from ashes....

But when the wave's tongue
washes away

death's warning
shot of adrenalin-

(happy,
the rest of us, just to be alive)

Steven Heighton

Address Book

Bad luck, it's said, to enter your own name
and numbers in the new address book.
All the same, as you slowly comb
through the old one for things to pick

out, transfer there, you are tempted to coin
yourself a sparkling new address,
new name, befitting the freshness of this clean-
slating, this brisk kiss

so long to the heart-renders—every friend
you buried or let drift, those Home for the Aged
maiden relations, who never raged
against the dying of anything, and in the end

just died. An end to the casualties pressed
randomly between pages—smudged, scribbled chits
with lost names, business cards with their faded
bold-fronts of confidence, solvency. The palimpsest

time made of each page; the hypocrite it made
of you. Annie, who you tried two years to love
because she was straight-hearted, lively, and in love
with you (but no strong-arming your cells and blood);

Mad Carl, who typed poet-to-poet squibs in the pseudo-
hickish, hectoring style of Pound, all sermonfire
and block caps, as AINT FIBRE ENOUGH HERE, BOYO,
BACK TO THE OLE FLAX FIELD . . . this *re* a score

of your nature poems. When he finally vanished
into the far east, you didn't mind the silence.
Still, this guilt, as if it weighs in the balance,
every choice—as if each time your pen banished

a name it must be sensed somewhere, a ballpoint stab, hex-
needle to the heart, the treacherous
innocent No of Peter, every X
on the page a turncoat kiss . . . .

Bad luck, it's said, to enter your own name in the new
book—as if, years on, in the next culling,
an executor will be leafing through and calling
or sending word to every name but you.

The Phone Never Rang

—like the silence of a friend with information
you know concerns you; stubborn secrecy.
On many days one is written to by no-one,
the door never unlocked. When Maurice Chevalier

finally cancelled his own conscious posterity
with an *aperitif* of pills, his man-servant
(of course, he had one) was put on record by
a few dailies: "Monsieur, he almost went

mad, waiting, wishing still to be cast. Small bits,
even! The phone never rang." *Every little breeze*

seems to whisper Louise. And how, as one sits
with a body after the blood's setting, in these

dens filling with dusk (where no one thinks of a light)
something old in each mourner still awaits a sigh
as lips end-rhyme some posthumous insight,
hint from a locked locale . . . . Think how Houdini,

dying, said, "Wait by my grave, Bess. If I can, I'm
going to reach you—though I suppose that's no safe
bet . . ." But then it's a given, the Silence of the Tomb;
the silence of the living brings deeper grief.

"Satchel Feet", the giant Primo Carnera—go ask
him, who never knew the mob bought him his title,
who withered from World Champion to asterisk
in a bell's knelling, who from his hospital

deathbed told a last, bored stringer for the *Tribune,*
"I haven't a friend in the world." Or Abishag,
ex-stroker of all King David's crowns, at last a crone
in the frost, swabbing steps with pail and rag—

she must have wondered why the palace never rang.
And last Tom, my friend, his books being forgotten
without malice, cold or casual—without even
our awareness—on your floor that last evening

as cicadas whined beyond like wires, skateboard-boys
clattered hard, and you helpless to rise, realizing
this event, too, would not be pillowed by praise—
how only friendship ever lessened the blows—

you must have wondered why your phone didn't ring.

David Helwig

The Wrong Side of the Park

—for Tom

In your last poem lie
elms by the courthouse cut
in an epoch of disease.
(The trees attend in their silence
the flight of a hurtful lover.)

A new elm risen in your name
stands three men high tonight
on the wrong side of the park.
(You camped eastward, on West
now in the obverse of living.)

In your crazed clairvoyant city
fearless children climb, who
explore a geography seen
from the back of the map.
(You are nowhere and with us.)

"human remains in Louisiana"

. . . and has come
apart, released
from its aim,
unrhymed by such force

that what was adored
is cryptic,
cracked dispatch, parsed
as cipher,

and what sky took, earth
awaits, as each one

but faster, sheath
of air burns,

sundered code rains
an atrocious manna.

L A Henry

My Uterus is the Hotel California

My uterus is the Hotel California:
you can check out
you can put in miles
walls of words
mazes, mosaics of meaning
shaping and defining yourself
as not me, but
bottom line
you can never leave.

Like the internal organ
my uterus balloons
to encompass all that you are
no matter how big
how distant you get
I can contain you
until,
the fire of birth
the knife of childbirth
cuts between us
the cord of emotion.

Born again, you are cold and alone
but
(though you do not know it)
my uterus has stretched yet again
and I still contain you.
You can never leave.

Frost

Frost
bitter fallen flakes, like
snow and leaves
like dandruff
on the wool blazered shoulders
black and smelling of closet space
of the young father.

Frost fell at night
and stayed all day
played out like a pale
burlesque movie star,
a clip run at the wrong speed
on an ancient projector.

Frost in the air
clinging, like a filthy film
on the windows of the red sports car
in the garage
abandoned by the father
(now pushing middle age
still sporting dandruff flakes
on his sweater).

Frost all winter
on the cornfields in Richmond
where a Christmas walk
turns into a bitter battle
stiletto emotions bayoneting
the veneer of festivity,
peeling normalcy back
to the ulcerated pain
of a twenty year old marriage.

The corn was crispy and golden
under the frost
and the ears dried, un-harvested
on the stalks
while the air hung
cool and blue.

Eileen Holland

Five Shovelfuls of Earth

My father, the son of an orchardist and produce farmer, inherited the love of gardening. The garden was Dad's painting, set on an easel a quarter of an acre in size. He dabbled at it constantly, changing colors, shapes, and textures on a regular basis. He nurtured it, deriving joy each spring when the sun, the rain, and the work of his hands caused life to burst forth. Summer's abundance, fall's harvest, and winter's anticipation rounded out his gardener's year.

I once made the mistake of suggesting where a hole for a new plant should be dug in the dirt. He turned to look at me, searching my face for understanding. "This isn't dirt, Eileen. This is earth."

His cherished earth, as if in appreciation, produced bush beans with more beans than bush and Swiss chard as thick as a man's forearm. It turned out tomatoes as red as a toddler's cheeks in winter, berries the size of plums, and apples so plentiful that the excess ended up in local soup kitchens. Woodland ferns edged the house, and dahlias chummed with roses, lilies and clematis in a charming English flower garden.

My father lived a rich, full life until his early sixties when my mother noticed that a raspiness had infiltrated his voice. Years of doctor's appointments turned up nothing. "Face it, John," stated one doctor. "You're just getting old." My father was offended. He gardened daily, climbed mountains, skied, and wind surfed.

A decade after the onset of his voice concerns, his speech had become so slurred he used a pad and pencil to convey his thoughts. One day, a diagnosis came through from a specialist who knew his business but lacked a bedside manner. "You've got A.L.S., John, commonly known as Lou Gehrig's Disease. You have two years to live." The blunt prognosis shocked everyone. It couldn't be true.

It was. Over the next few months, his voice deteriorated into indecipherable grunts and whispers. Swallowing became a chore and finally a G-tube was inserted as choking during meals became too hazardous.

Through all of this, he continued gardening. In his garden, his garbled speech was inconsequential, his struggle to survive, unimportant. Comfort was drawn from the grate of soil against shovel, the rustle of birds in the bushes, the whisper of an armful of leaves.

In his seventy-sixth year, involuntary twitches in his limbs signaled the arrival of the weakness destined to overtake his body. He became painfully thin and unable to garden for more than a few minutes. One day I saw him enter the garden with a pair of clippers. He snipped one branch off a bush, stood looking at the garden for five minutes, and returned inside.

My brothers and sister and I stepped up our assistance with the more difficult gardening, spelling off our mother. One day I went out to edge a flowerbed in the front garden, this particular spot being heavy with clay. It was a windy day. My hair kept blowing across my eyes, blinding me to my task. I was hacking up the earth with the edge of my spade when I glimpsed a movement through the wisps of my hair.

It was my father. With his six-foot-one frame weighing in at a gaunt ninety-seven pounds, he listed, rather than walked, toward me. He glided forward with his mouth hanging open, his jaw muscles no longer receiving messages from his brain, having given up. Unable to speak, unable to command a smile to his face, he locked eyes with me and grunted softly in greeting.

"Hi, Dad," I replied, but my heart dropped into the pit of my stomach at the sight of what he held in his hands.

It was a shovel. This man, with days to live, had come out to help with the gardening. He carried it before him in both hands, like a child holds the string of a helium balloon, his arm muscles unable to imitate the nonchalance with which a healthy man would have borne it.

Carefully he placed the shovel into the earth and stepped down on the tread. The blade dug in and my father stooped to turn the soil.

Words tumbled forward in my mind. "Dad, you'll overdo it. What are you thinking?"

I couldn't speak those words. The moment belonged to him. He was standing in the good earth where he belonged, wielding a shovel alongside his daughter. As long as he had breath remaining, he'd share the weight of beautifying his domain.

Voices from the street distracted me. Three teenage girls were walking by. Hoots of laughter, jokes, and playful shoving punctuated their passing. They looked like whirlwinds as the breeze whipped their open coats and flared pants about their developing bodies. A fleeting glance was cast in our direction, taking in the sick old man digging by his daughter's side. Then we were forgotten, as they walked on into the lives stretching before them.

My breath came out clipped into short, painful gasps. I wanted to run after them and say, "See my father in his final hours, making such an effort. Isn't he something?" But instead I kept digging, as my father did by my side.

My dad turned five shovelfuls of earth that day. Then he went back into the house.

Several days later, he slipped gradually into a coma and died peacefully in his sleep. When news of his passing came to me, I remembered a comment he had made when he could no longer speak. On a scrap of paper he had written, "How I hate to leave this lovely world."

Throughout my life I have seen people, stricken by sickness, loneliness, or grief, who stopped living, years before they actually died. They sat in chairs or lay in beds, trapped in their own despair. Dad wanted my last memory of him to be of a man determined to the end, no matter the obstacles. It was his final triumph, as if he clamped a hand on my backbone that day and made it strong and straight. Message taken, Dad.

Cornelia Hoogland

Orange Insect

I read in the paper that McLuhan the great
Canadian media guru
after the eighteen-hour surgery
to remove a brain tumor the size of a tennis ball
at the base of his skull
curiously almost perversely remembered
his abiding passion for the songs of Harry Lauder
a Scottish tenor he hadn't given a moment's thought
in the intervening years.

The intervening years.

McLuhan's *medium-is-the-message* trickled down
into our collective like snow, like
the orangey Asian ladybugs

imported for the Soya bean crop but flying
into saucepans, bedsheets, up shirt sleeves
all summer. I don't know much about McLuhan
but I do know about brain surgery,
about my son's twenty-four hour surgery–it never making the paper.

I'm thinking that after Cameron's operation
all the great new thoughts he might have had
were gone.

McLuhan regained a Scottish tenor
squirming sideways like an insect
through a summer screen,
and Cameron–maybe he also gained.
I curiously almost perversely try to imagine
that minutiae of possibility
in my eighteen year-old son's magnificent loss.

As I write this poem an orange ladybug
moon-walks over my mouse pad.
Stops to wash her feelers one with the other
like chopsticks crossed. I watch.
It's like she's waving. At me.

Paying attention is the only
thing any of us can do.
But the verb *pay* is right.
It costs. It costs everything.

Gary Hyland

Your Name

You are the saying of your name
and the silences before and after
your name is said. There is none
of these without the other and all
are the spell which happens to me
whenever your name

is spoken. Wild geese, like one wing,
vanish through clouds, reappear.
Geese, clouds, the pale spaces
between are the vision
I fall into as the brook enters
a stream when I hear

your name spoken I slide
into one of the ways you are in me
and move out and apart on a song
of longing as one who roams
unconcerned far into a forest
to receive the music at

its heart. Your name is you
awakening me deep in this
valley where the sun kindles hills
of cherry blossoms and their light
spills into my eyes and their scent
fills me.

Adjusting

Your father and mother do
not die. It is always your
Mom and Dad
you cry for.

No matter what lie
you need to tell yourself,
you are the last
alone and that's not
good. No chance now
for final

healings. The man in Group
who plays your Dad
gets what's wrong
all wrong.

The graveside chats with Mom
the therapist advised
give you sunburn.

Welcome
to the orphanage.
You can hang your photos
anywhere you like

Afternoon, Crescent Park

Near the minnow pond
where I fished as a boy I watch
a girl build walls of mud,
adding twigs, pebbles leaves.
An old man, her grandfather
perhaps, flecked with shade,
sits on a bench nearby. They
are from an oriental land,
one that might now be called
the former this or former that.

Gazing at the girl's work,
forehead gleaming, wisps of white
hair straying in the breeze,
he rests as though in dream
on the bamboo cane between
his legs, chin on his hands.
Leans from tree-filtered traffic
towards her lopsided walls.

Once she pats the mud in place
the furious heat hardens it
fast into the shape they might
recognize, a hut in a cluster
of huts that looks like a past
they cannot revisit or revise.

Audrey

In memory of Audrey Johannessohn

Her massive hand crushed mine
as she boomed
"Well, I've heard good things about you,"
then looked me up and down,
"but they musta been lies."

She never drove a rig but could have,
waited on tables in a border town,
salt and pepper shakers
trembling when she lumbered past,
listening to the truckers' laments,
giving her tips to runaway girls.

"Had me a fifty-buck make-over once.
Looked like a goddamned movie star.
But who ever dates Lassie?"

Her cure for melancholy bards:
Stomp into a crowded lounge and roar,
"Hey, poet, you'd better thank me big time.
I saved your life a minute ago."
"How?" I ask warily.
"Ran over a shit-eating dog."

It was stupid when she died,
I couldn't help thinking,
Who's going to save me now?

Beth Janzen

Letter to Corinth

I. Hotel Acti

My mother wouldn't stay here.

A hall of dust and broken tile,
a stab of blue, an iron railing.
The view is sheets and a rusted ladder.
One mosquito on the ceiling.

II. The Park

Three to a bench, the women in black
cross themselves to the lull of bells.

We sulk unbelieving in our tainted clothes.
For that Laundromat, we'd bussed
8 hours. We brood on our night of barking
dogs, the scourge of scooters. Palm trees
can't console us.

> Then a child stands in yellow shoes.
> She sees my thoughts and they astound her.
> One time, two, she lifts her hands
> > mouths a kiss

> *If I have not love*
> *I have nothing*

and I love this:
> hot pastry on this aching morning
> boats fanned wide in the Bay of Corinth
> wet socks and underwear clipped to a string
> the simplicity in every thing.

Joanne Jefferson

A Separate City

—(for my brother)

I chased your ghost for months
before you'd even died. Tried
to argue against your leaving, tried
to prove myself to you, to make something
more than intimate nostalgia
in separate cities.

I always felt the decade between us;
afraid to wake you on the bus,
afraid to spark your skeptical wit, waiting
for you to lift me high like you
did when I was four and five, the only
times I touched the ceiling.
Chronology governed us.

I needed to ask, *would it still?*
Would you still ignore me,
stick your face in a book, chew your thumb?
Would you still laugh at my
ears, twist my arm, write me long letters?
Would you still find my lovers
more intriguing than me?

I almost caught you
that night we walked a dark beach road
starved for moonlight, trusting
the luminescent surf. You told me
you'd considered suicide but
I didn't understand what you
said had changed your mind,
made you wait
for some slower end.

I had time for only one more visit
and rode the train for two days
to sleep in your spare room, to eat
with your buoyant friends.
We navigated your neighbourhood
like old acquaintances;
an awkward reunion, uncertain
of boundaries.

Now, I recognize you everywhere:
my son's long feet, a stranger's gait,
the size of your laugh. I find
your hands at the ends of my arms,
find words for
what you might have seen.

Widowhood

—(in homage to Donal Linehan, 1924-2003)

The day of his funeral it snowed.
And snowed. Proper, somehow, as if
he'd wished this mischief on us, settling
white and even on the headstones,
soft feathers in the grave.

Through the dimming hours we sat
together, every face repeating
a phrase of his—sister's eyebrow,
daughter's cheekbone, grandchildren laughing
from room to room. And still
the house was empty as the world
disappearing in snow and grieving.

Near midnight I stepped out
for a quiet minute, the snow falling
simply, and someone walking
along the road. Male or female, I couldn't tell
but I knew the figure carried
his ghost like the cloak of snow.
He'd borrowed the muffled night for passing.

Gail Johnston

Vestigium

For Debra

Sites of old amputations on the curly-leafed apple tree,
suckers, carefully pruned, year after year, healed over,
look now like breasts: dappled, blossom-sized mounds
with pursed nipples. Good for nothing, really, like mine
- perhaps vestigium, also, for what good are breasts
with no time to feed babies or no babies to feed or no time?
Besides, if this tree's any indication, old ones don't bear good fruit.

Sisters, forget implants or reductions.
After a double mastectomy,
get the surgeon to graft on limbs, instead;
show me a woman who couldn't use a spare pair
of hands, nowadays.

Deirdre Kessler

Light from the Hallway

Later she tells me I was a good baby, so good,
neighbours did not know I was there.
We live on Long Lane, our house attached to others
like a train curving down a slope of city.
Neighbours know my curly-haired brother,
two and a half when I come home from the hospital
with his mother. And they know my sister,
eleven, the one, they whisper,
who has a different father and maybe
the father of curly-head does not like her.

I am six months old, asleep in an almost-dark room.
Everything is familiar—every night the narrow path
of light falls across the floor the same way
and goes the same way up the wall. My eyes
are heavy, too heavy to keep her by me.
Sleep steals me, almost carries me away.
I see her retreat, light widening, narrowing
to the familiar pattern across the floor, up the wall.
She is never far away. I am happy. I let go.

Now I cry awake. My arm, my leg—I roll away
from the pain, pull myself to hands and knees.
A growl. Growling. I stare through the slats.
There is nothing but the terrifying sound.
Something behind me grabs my leg, holds on.
I shriek. The door opens to light and closes again,
but she is not here. Again I wail, and she appears,
sweeps me to her arms, comforts me, rocks me.

Sleep is irresistible, but the next night,
when she retreats, my eyes stay open.
The swath of light widens, closes.
The growl, the pincer, the shriek. The light
widens, closes. She does not come. Then the room
fills with light. She sweeps me up, presses me close.
She stays longer the next night, sings,
leaves the door wide open. I sleep.

"I am a lion. I am going to eat you."
Only tone and pain do I understand. Not words.
It grabs and holds my side, twists the flesh.
Before I can scramble away, the overhead light
is on and my mother has grabbed the monster
under the crib, pulled him out. She turns her voice
hard to him. "You may not do this. She is a baby.
You may not scare her or hurt her. Do you understand?"
His face contorts. He cries. That beautiful head nods;
curls of an angel. How has he fallen so far from grace?

She picks me up, comforts me, tells me there is
no monster, nothing to fear. He is sorry. All is well.
I understand relief in her voice: the good baby
crying for no reason. We walk him together
to his room, see him into his bed, covered.
And I have learned something: how to sleep
in the middle of my crib, exactly in the middle,
where no monster can grab ahold of my fat little self.
And I have learned how to raise the living with a
scream. Later, my brother apologizes. He is thirty
and has a curly-haired baby of his own, one
who likes the light left on when he sleeps.

That Story

I am five and these things fit together:
Brer Rabbit and the Tarbaby—poor Brer Rabbit
kicking that rude Tarbaby, getting his furry self
all stuck in the tar. And we live next door
to a highways storage yard: heaps of sand and
cinders for winter, a wall of stacked cans of tar
for patching summer roads. Perfect, sun-warmed
tar spilled on concrete, bubbling up, cooling
down at night. Dribbles and globs. Half-used
cans with lids askew. We roll that tar
round ball, round ball in our little hands,
push it with the toes of our sneakers. I eat some—
the seductive temperature and texture of it
between my fingers, then tar in my mouth and
I understand how touch and taste are different.
Tar and Brer Fox's trick on Brer Rabbit
are rolled together with one more thing:
sure knowledge of how to escape.
Brer Rabbit tells Brer Fox, "Oh, whatever you do,
jes' doan throw me in dat briarpatch!"
What does Brer Fox do? He pitches that rabbit
into that briarpatch. Yes, Brer Rabbit lands
smack-dab in the middle of his briary home.

I am tenting in an oasis in Death Valley.
It is thirty years later. Shade from desert sun
in the cool of willows along a creek is my escape
from winter in Prince Edward Island.
Tent, bird book, journal. I am happy.
Mornings I jog; afternoons I hike ten kilometers
to a mineral spring; nights, there's dancing
at a rough bar, but I slip out the back door
before the ugly stuff starts. No one knows
who I am or where I camp. That's what I think.
This night, I doze under stars on a flat rock
by my campfire a distance from the hidden tent.
Midnight at the oasis. Then they come roaring
into the canyon in pickup trucks, gun
engines up the rutted track towards the creek.
I am standing, kicking sand over the coals,
running back towards the tent. And then I see
how easily found a northern girl is; how obvious

the campsite; how clear from months of sidelong
scrutiny at the bar what is about to unfold.
But I remember a story. I know this thatch
of willow and salt cedar, creosote bush and mesquite.
I grab my pack from the tent: passport, wallet, journal,
water bottle. I creep into the thicket, keep going,
push with my soft-skinned hands and face
through the underbrush; crouch, crawl—and now
I am home. Smack-dab in the middle.

Norman G. Kester

writing to remember

Your face wrinkled by tortured rivers of time.
Your stomach filled with bitter snakes.
"I fell *naar,*" you once told me
only for your frightened *boetie* to forget misery's companion.
The casket craves for love.
Your body bleeds of madness, exile.
I remember that jersey, mildewed with your body's
secret scent—a story, a sonnet that shared poverty's cruel hand.
I felt your silent tears cut
right through me like time's bloody knife.
It is I who fled this lonely life, not thee.

I love to dance and sing
black songs that feed madness' frenzied heart.
I sleep I dream I kill I die
Dead babies do not cry.
The poet is father to his nation's horrors.
My father's guilt is my ma's sorrow.
I'd like to go
and lie beside her brave bones.
Lakes of loss. Lands of black shame.

Women's painful beauty
paint my world.
It is their eyes that haunt
me beautifully as my mother's dead body
sleeps beside me.
Her jealousy and rage are *lekker*
to the ear, *né.* I write her
songs and shed the same tears
that she cried in her childless fear.
War is man's folly. Fame, his misfortune.

John B. Lee

Gathering Stone for the Garden

The day my grandfather fell in the field
his heart was a stone
drumming the boat
with an almost fatal drop
of final granite
as he lay down on the low wood of the bed
and chirped the horse
for the house, for he was hurt
when they dragged him home
with the frost heave
his round belly cold as a clay furrow
his forehead gone grey as hard land
and though he did not die that day
under that particular heaven
the slack-lined horses
nickered the calm
and his daughters walked the earth after
where it was not mallow
when I was but a barely born boy
the phone rang in the den
as the cruel news came.

And now, I am almost fifty
and on the same farm
with my wife
who is gathering garden beauty
from an accidental cairn
after we've walked the weedy corn
ankle thistled and mean
coming here
to stand under the dead-limbed elm
at the centre of summer.

I am climbing the clack and rumble
gathered in time by the man who fell
to ground
I am turning in my hands
some of those same stones
I am holding the heavy-hearted land
nudging at sorrow
finding my place in the plough-toughened time
setting the clock of sparrows
in the portulaca, the nasturtium
and the priest-black hollyhock
high as my hands
I am setting the clock
of the smoke bush
and the lily
as the season comes softly
touching the stone
like a cousin waking an uncle
for supper
when the uncle has died in his sleep.

The Lost Knife

My father let his own father
go
without telling him
the secret
concerning the loss of the pocket knife.

Every year
Herb went to Chicago
to show sheep
and in the twenties
he took whiskey
to slake the thirsty city
"where's that big Irishman
from Canada?"
they'd say, each wanting his dram

from when the stock car first arrived
and the sheep came tripping
down the ramp
shaking their wools like a dozen well-made mops
with him behind them.

And he traded
one Walkers's amber whiskey bottle
for a dozen knives
from Jack-Knife Benny
one for Ben, several as gifts
and the best bone-handled blade
he kept for himself
folded hard in his pocket
like a second masculine danger.

Then, much later
one day in early June
he sent his son George
armed and sharp with that weapon
to the wheat to cull tall rye
cut by cut
and boy soon grew bored
and lay in the green
tossing and seeking in circles of whereabouts
until it was lost
in sixteen acres of spring-shot wheat.

What to tell father?
Oh, he was a clever lad—
so he cut a hole
in his pocket with his own tiny gift
and then walked
up the long lane to the barn.

"Are you done, boy?
Where's my knife—"
and the lad, patting his leg
like a theft
pulled out the cut cotton

saying, "I must've lost it.
See the hole, dad?"
And his thus-cousined father
touched the place of the liar
like a kirk of the tartan
lamenting the loss.

Meanwhile, this seventy-eight-year-old man
my own father
shares the secret with me
saying, "Dad went to his grave
never knowing…"
and he smiles at the mischief
the clever deceit
at the ghost of a knife
still open
and seeking his dead father's hand.

Malca Litovitz

Splintering

In the night, I awake
 to the vast silence—
the truth splintering:
is it truth or fear?
the marriage shattered
like a board cracked over our heads—
the bed no longer squeaking
with passion.

"Do you still love me?"

"Yes".

"This is how we fell asleep."

I rest my head on his shoulder,
 entwine my legs with his.

"Do you still love me?"

I sigh and open the window
to peer out on the dark street,
to feel air caress my face.

Post surgery

Upon waking from anaesthetic,
I call for a brass-tack man, who loves me,
but the cavern in my groin, abdominal rip-up,
is the pain you left
when you tore yourself from me—

my bladder, fused to my uterus, ripped a little—
the way my heart tore
when you stood to leave me.

Ecuador

I want to get your letter
from Ecuador again
(you love every inch of my being)
it arrives with barely an address
in the middle of the summer
smoulders in the mailbox

for me, unknown Señorita

in a red hot skirt

I throw it away

relive it

want to get your letter forever.

Hugh MacDonald

Triptych: a response to Bruno Bobak's *Wheel of Life*

1.
Is this all there is:
these awkward waves
of light and colour
these crude impressions
this naive unkempt
book of revelations
this rolling layered
perplexing mound
of flesh and bone
each and all born
into the world
prepared to suck
and wail and grasp?
And so it goes
the whole life long
filling up
and taking hold
of all we can
in the name of love
or other earlthly causes.
Or so we claim
despite the gaudy signs
and ugly scars
that mark our passage
through the lush landscapes
of this painted ball.

2.
He hadn't thought of her
in months
no rueful backward
looks, no penitential

shedding of self
no kneeling at the headstone
of their long buried love
in the bone yard of youth
leaving to others
the gleaning of their story
from such scant statistics
as the births and deaths
on the mossy faces
of pocked and faded stone
in the neglected cemeteries
they liked to wander
warm Sunday afternoons.
Let others analyze
the short fiction
of their learner marriage
that slow revealing
process
of discovering
who they really weren't
watching their naive
shades of green
bleed to faded bone.
   He mentioned parting.
The stroke was cruel.
Her hurt slammed her
to the floor
surprised him
seared like white-hot lead.
And so they blew apart
bits of themselves
buttered the landscape
staining everyone they knew
while their souls
tried to die.
But still they lived
and with passing time
signs of hope returned:
She found a good man

more suited to the life
she always dreamed to live
and he found love
strong enough
to hold his devils down
and years slipped by.
They spoke from time
to time and did their best
with kids, on friendly terms
always and fair.
               And then
one day somewhere past
the expected middle
of her time, he learned
how she was gravely ill
and nothing could be done
but say good-bye.
Their children at her side
she swallowed
noble death in days
and was no more.
               Deep inside him
something stirred
and darkness
dropped
down
hard.
               Pools dammed up
behind his eyes
and broke
and dried.
Looking back
her phantom face
pillared him
in salt.
He saw
the way she'd
been when love
was fresh

and all of that
was dead except
their two strong sons
and a thousand
small
regrets.

3.
Was there once
a better planned design
yet something in the paint
went wrong?
But we are old
before we learn our flaws
dying and our children
have no ears
for mournful warnings
from the nearly gone.
So I am moved
when I behold
this stormy sea
of dancing colours.
Before my eyes
the scene (like life)
redraws itself
and fills me up
with fear
and comfort both—
the truth of why I am
and not content
whatever helps and harms
that I dispense—
hoping someone's there
to hold me
in the final frame
and love me
though she can't recall
my name.

Steve McCabe

Down Grand Avenue in December

and I returned a minor poet
My mother's final breath too short
Two short bursts
I told the nurses, "She's still warm."
And they showed me the missing zig-zags on the cardiac strip
And one touched my shoulder
And the vessel of beating heart pumping blood afloat on the Nile
Sent me into the world in a little wicker psyche.
At winter concerts she walked to the bank I never knew how
Proud wearing my silver tinsel collar on a white gown she sewed
We Three Kings of Orient are going down to the hospital
Cafeteria later to the hotel twisting another cork free
Brothers and sisters *by gawd* hell raisers;
"Yes it is serious, Mrs. McCabe."
The cigarettes finally surrounding you in their cloud of constriction
Contamination and cremation
Your ashes mailed to Oregon one final jaunt across the dance floor
As if you were piloting the plane.
I talk to you looking at photographs
Enormous me growing inside
Here you are dying I stroke your hair one final time
Returning home a minor poet.

Death Certificate

A photograph of where you last lived
The surprise length of time...
A photograph of brothers and sisters
Since you were diagnosed...
A photograph beside the pool
With what killed you...
Kneeling inside your closet

And you denying always denying...
And for twelve hours beside you
That it caused any harm...
There I am inside your womb
As if you were invincible...
Here I am half-a-century later
I too expected you to go on forever...
After half a day stroking your brow
To never go away...
Holding your hand
To not leave me an orphan...
Thanking you Mother
To perpetually bring me into the world...
Loving you Mother
To never be that much older than me...
Young in a black and white photograph
To never be laid down...

Robin McGrath

Elegy For a Tired Old Dog

The sun rises from the ocean like a pease-pudding
From a boiled dinner, the harbour steams,
Sending everyone to the beaches and ponds,
Sending a sheepdog and his mistress to the banks of
Long Pond, the haunt of skating parties and skiers,
Bird watchers and berry pickers, where even an old dog
Can find relief from the heat of a record-breaking summer.
Winston walks cumbrously to the shore, his old hips
Protesting the distance, his disobedient feet stumbling
As his nose drops from habit to catch the scent of
Other dogs, too stiff to lift his leg, though.
"C'mon Winston, in you go," his mistress calls.
Winston hesitates and sighs, raises his head.
"C'mon Winston," the swimmers shout, splashing,
And even the other dogs glance towards him, sending

Telepathic canine messages his way.
Ducks and children, and a lone osprey
fishing for trout at the reedy end of the pond.
Cry shrill, piercing encouragement, "C'mon Winston!"
The bones of cattle from Halliday's farm,
The invisible lines of Noad's survey maps, and even
The ghosts of Bob Bartlett's Eskimo dogs who pulled
Huge blocks of ice at Grandpa's Christmas parties,
All holler out encouragement: "C'mon Winston,
In you go Winnie boy, time for a swim, old fellow."
But he just lurches, stiff legged, in up to his knees,
And turns blind, clouded eyes towards the shore.
He is hot and panting, but too tired to cool off,
Exhausted by the noise and the unfamiliar footing.
A dog who is tired of Long Pond is tired of life,
Someone said, time for the going-away party,
The appointment with the big vet in the sky.
Next summer when a new pup comes to the pond,
Another voice will be added to the old ones,
A youthful Winston bark: "C'mon boy, in you go,"
Then it's off with Captain Bob, on another adventure,
A trip to the North Pole, or near as makes no matter.

An Immigrant's Geography

The title catches my eye, black letters on a green field,
A tiny caribou head at the base of the spine,
Wheaton's Newfoundland Geography, the text I had in grade six,
Poured over in class and at night, read cover to cover,
Imports, exports, the work of the Buchans miner,
Labrador floaters with their summer catch
Sailing down the coast in glorious triumph,
A map of Canada with tiny planes and trains
Criss-crossing the mountains and prairies.
I turned the pages of that book
While sitting in my father's greenhouse,
Eating tomatoes off the vine and carelessly
Dropping grains of salt into the binding.

This copy is annotated in a child's hand.
I puzzle my way through the German
As she stumbled through the English.
>   The First Settlement: *Die ersten Andiedlungen*
>   Sea Treasures: *See Schatze*
>   Before the White Men Came: *Bevor die weißen Kamen*
>   Under a photograph of a woman in a parka: *Das ist ein Eskimo*
And folded into the back, a word list, the German in an older hand
>   Seal—*Seehund*
>   Hunt—*Jagd*
>   Industry—*Fabrik Ports Hafen*
>   Codfishery—*Dorschfischerei*
Some words on the list are not translated:
>   Secretly—
>   Remained—
>   Life—
>   Place to Live—
>   Home—

There is salt in the spine of this book too,
Salt tears for the lost language, the geography of the heart.

---

rob mclennan

milk

the carcass of the old house after she moved
to the apartment. damp,
& rot. was the only one i know who made
tomato soup w/

milk, the cloudy white stirrd in

slowly, continuous. uncle bob crushing premium plus
w/ his spoon. renovated the kitchen & back after

husband died, his winter body brought in

after discovery in the snow, lay there cold
& stiff on the table

until the ambulance arrived, knowing
they neednt hurry. this much

is sure, is what

i know, how long

years can reach out thru, from
behind & grab

at your neck like you were seven a second time,
scanning magazines in the wrong part

of another uncles house, black marks

over the parts of the female anatomy you knew,
even then, were interesting.

nothing in particular, all the time

—(an alberta train poem, for frances

steam rises
from the surface of the lake

in victoria, where she says
even the infrequent rain is warm

everyone is neither happy, nor sad

looking forward to the cold
of a return to ontario

three long years

nearly forgot the fog
that breath makes, on cold glass

w/ her index, marks
a single F

on the death of paterson ewen

this is a light, a
cloth

& goes by temporarily

a mark made deep, a gouge
in wood panel

"portraying sweeping vistas"

of distinction, & goes by
so

remarkably rare

unscathed, undecorated
for but a year

halleys star, bare stretches
widening blue

for good or bad,
a moment

increasing in demand
& density

Christina McRae

Outdone

I found you sad and couldn't let it be
offered words, arms, breasts of compassion
and you suckled

nuzzling my neck in the kitchen you whispered
(while your penis poked and bumped)
that you never loved her like this

I smiled over a cringe and withering
shifting between the wool itch of your sweater
and the sharp edge of counter in my back

I said you can't help what you feel
it's what you do that counts
not believing a word of it

I wanted to find in your loss
a memory I couldn't cheapen
something I couldn't outdo

Too often now

we say nothing
after lovemaking the yes-but-now-what feeling
stifles endearments
your body alongside mine like warm still water

Wives sulk in marriages made by children
engage in Tupperware chat, choose kitchen tile
men work too much, just to feel *something*
if only boot-dead fatigue

When I get sad, I stay sad for weeks
collect arguments, listen only to myself
trying to come up a new beginning
or better ending

I want a harder love

For Iain turning five

When you were lost last summer
somewhere between the road, Fort Anne, and the sea
the landscape turned desolate, lifeless
and the view from every hill and bank I raced up and over
came up empty
I screamed your name like a mad incantation
to bring you back, to place you there

every direction turned up a crime scene
I pictured your little boy body
crumbled in a dusty heap by the side of the road
the driver mistaking the size and thump for a dog
and driving on
or worse, you snatched and shoved into that same grey car
seatbelt-less, rattling around the hard box of the backseat
noticed by no one, miles away going God knows where

there's no space emptier than where you were
but love stays
fills places to overflowing

today in the house it reaches upstairs
to the terrycloth mouse left sleeping on your pillow
to the sticky circle on the dresser where you put down your juice
all the way to the bottom of the hamper
to those balled-up socks ringed with dirt and a red stripe

it hovers around the kitchen couch
where I've watched you somersault
heard you laugh till you toppled over
seen you drag the seat cushion up the stairs
for the wild ride down

and love's there with the milk in your Rice Krispie bowl
at the backdoor left open behind you

I found you ten minutes later
stuck, ankle-deep in the sludge before the sea
you'd gone to feel how warm the water was

and despite the world turning and all of time
love was particular to the mud on your white sneakers
to the round fat pudge of your check
the sweet-salt smell of your neck
to your arms and legs wrapped tight around my panic
how can I ever let you go?

What can stillness bring?
Who will I be when you're gone?

Dianne Hicks Morrow

Same Old Story

Your Great Grandfather cleared this land
out of the wilderness with an axe and saw,
all one hundred acres of it.
Your Grandfather made this furniture with a few hand tools.
Never see his like again.

That's my father speaking, wistfully,
as though that farm is the place he'd really like to be.
He left there at fourteen to work in the lumberwoods.
Later came the gold mine in Timmins, the war,
and the Newfoundland girl who became my mother.
She knew she never wanted to be a farmer's wife.
He said he didn't want to take over his father's farm
any more than his eight brothers and sisters did.

Father ran a portable sawmill,
made gunstocks and snowshoes.
We grew all our own food.
Wild game got us through the winter
but the smoked ham from the pig we raised
was what we looked forward to most.

How I wish I'd taped Dad's voice
because now he's been gone nearly a year
and already I'm forgetting details.
Was it sauerkraut they *put down cellar* in a barrel?
And how did they make soap?
Wish I'd never yawned and whispered to Mom
"Oh no, here he goes again."

Father ground all our flour.
Mother baked a dozen loaves of bread at a time.
Never less than a dozen of us to feed at a meal, you know.

Seed Planting

Funny what makes me cry:
leftover Vesey's Seeds
your farmer's fingers will never sow,
the guestbook from The Roost
with your misspelled notations on weather,
tides and deaths in the back.
Your La-Z-Boy upholstery darkened
by the warmth of your legs,
sits in the cold basement of my mother-in-law
waiting for your grandson to make a home for it.

My house is bursting with your past.
The lamps you made from black cherry your father bought
for gunstocks his one trip to the States.
His oak dresser and washstand adorn my guest room.
The mahogany china cabinet you made for your bride
stands in my hall now, filled with fifty-four years of marriage.
You made these coasters with spruce slices from my husband's woodlot.
You taught me that material things don't matter,
but if your hands made it I can't let go.

These seeds, I now remember, were bought
by my husband to plant your last garden for you.
On a day pass from the hospital you hobbled
into that garden to pull weeds we missed.
We laughed then, but you were gone before the harvest.

Kit Pepper

Empty and Full

I have a photo of my youngest son, he's 5 or 6
T-shirt on backward and inside out, ear to ear grin
I can't see his feet in this picture

but my friend tells me he always wore shoes
three sizes too big and it's probably true—
wanting from the start to be grown like his brothers.
When I tell him now both are proud of him
he says he wouldn't be who he is
without those two. And I think it *is* the lot of the third
to be so influenced—waters pulled—two brothers
holding him first when he was born
then handing him to me.
Now his youngest son wants to move
into his oldest brother's bedroom, sleep amongst
posters of pyramids and the Taj Mahal.
My first-born set out his life, showed what was to come
in pictures, like what a clairvoyant might see
in a crystal ball. Seems we all move through our lives
in different ways, some pulled by pictures or siblings,
others by instinct that something is right,
will carry us closer to who we are or want to be.
And this youngest son wants to be as close as possible
to brothers who have left,
left rooms that are empty.
and full.

Marilyn Gear Pilling

Confetti-Tumbling Night

You put more lipstick on your full red lips
that night and I said, You won't be able to kiss
anyone if you don't blot your lips, and you said,
I leave my lips unblotted on purpose, I like to leave
my mark on men; there's hardly a man in this town
hasn't worn my red lips at one time or another.

From the beginning I wanted to marry you,
my sister, eight years younger, you were always
a wild girl, always a smart girl too, you could learn

whatever your big sister chose to teach you—
how to type, at age four, how to recite
at age six *The Rhyme Of The Ancient Mariner,*
how to drive, at age eight, the narrow back road
to town, how to cross the river where you couldn't
be seen from the house. It was to be on the river,
our wedding, water slap slapping the side
of the boat, the boat tip tipping, our feet
slosh sloshing. It was to be August, a night
like the summer nights we played tickle-
minnowed in the river's endless furl and babble.

In your teens you sold drugs from the basement
of the library, shimmied up the silo, soused,
in your bikini, traveled the world and welcomed
the stranger to your bed. Grown up, you became
a doctor. That red-lipsticked night, you went
to the hospital party, wearing your Carmen dress
with the deeply V'd back. Dared by a colleague
you left the table, returned with your dress
on backwards, V revealing you to the navel,
waist-length hair a swaying beckoning curtain.
Oh yes, small town lips buzzed the next day,
incisors vibrated, molars shuddered in their own
spew, jaws needed soldering.

You had parties at your own house that made
foundations judder. The night of our mother's
funeral you held a wake they heard across the river.
Your partner, the third one, made steaks
at midnight, those of us not too sloshed to sit up
sat with our elbows on the table tearing meat
from the T bone cross with our teeth, quaffing
the liquid fire you poured with profligacy.
When our father died ten weeks later you cried
enough tears to float him all the way to the hereafter—
never mind the ferryman, none was needed.

Always I wanted to marry you, my sister,
thought once our parents were gone
you'd be mine at last. Instead, it was then

that you found him, hair burning gold
like our father's, slight, with our father's fine
bones, our father's blue eyes spilling fire.
You put away the lipsticked nights and the drink,
put away the deep V's and the parties, announced,
one bright morning, your intention to turn this stranger
into husband, turning me into jealous jilted suitor.

Always I dreamed us an August wedding,
a night sultry, close, water slap
slapping the side of the boat, us tip tippling,
all of us so swizzled with tipple juice
that when the minister asks whether anyone
knows any reason why this woman and this woman
should not be joined in holy matrimony
my husband does not say Because one of them
is married to me already, and my daughter
does not say Because one of them is my Mommy,
and the man on the right does not say
Because both of them are women, a night
so charmed not one mosquito dares to whine
when the minister asks that question,
and when he proclaims that the bride may now kiss
the bride, we fall into one another's arms, topple
over the side of the boat into the starshining
river and swim as one into the confetti-tumbling night.

Barbara Rager

Waiting for Better Light

Then, in the Tantramar spring we tore off our gloves
And stroked the frozen marshland floor with our hot skin.
Buds burst from their cradles, blossomed and fluttered like fingers
Dancing to the carnival tunes in our heads.
We ran, clapping like seagulls, down the tambourine road to Fundy Bay,
Leaving your untouched canvass in the dark, to wait for better light.

But even then, even with the smell of turpentine tickling the air of a new day,
I fell back again into your paint-spattered arms,
And we stretched like waves across the dawning light of the summer morning.
Now, in Montreal, the autumn air holds our breath in a crisp suspension between us.
I see the leaves of our vigour and young madness curl and drop like paper.
And the verdant truths we had stapled on those canvass frames,
The blooming world we had held in our bare hands and raised to the laughing sun,
Lie twisted in the dry branches of a dying tree.
Lusterless and self-crucified, stretched against the setting light of the winter evening.

Lloyd Ratzlaff

Compline

Summer 1956. When Saskatoon's skyline is the Robin Hood flour mill and the smoking funnel of the Bessborough Hotel, when the popcorn man stands with his red cart at the corner of Avenue B and 20th Street under the awning of Adilman's store, and the eastbound Supercontinental takes on passengers in the heart of the city, and whistles and pulls away, out in the country there is a dugout beside a poplar bush, and in the center of the bush a little hideout that is the safest place on earth.

To get there, we have to cross a pasture at my cousins' farm, keeping one eye on a fearsome bull in the corner of the fence, and the other watching for cow pies in the grass. Safely past, we come to four cement slabs, as big as the bases of statues, leading into the dugout: the first lies flat on the prairie, the second tilts down a bit, the third is half in and half out of the water, and the last one knee-deep in the dugout, with a raft tied to a post beside it. The farthest pad shimmers underwater in the sun, and beyond it are mud and weeds and murky depths.

Today my cousin and I are here with a Rogers syrup pail, catching things from the dugout, mostly snails and tadpoles. She dips, pulls out five snails. Slippery in our fingers, we scoop them out, fat little pointy black pears. And line them up on the cement.

My turn. I lean over the water, and fetch up three more. We throw the tadpoles back. Six snails make an L—four down and two across; twelve snails for two Ls, one for Lorraine, one for Lloyd.

A calf bawls beside the fence. The cow butts it away. A cricket begins to hum, and sings along the barbed wire until it peters out.

Lorraine's turn again, nine shiny snails this time. She's getting good at it, enough for an O and one left over for an R.

How many snails spell our names?

Ripples from the dugout lap faintly on the concrete. The grass is fresh. A girl smells good, better than her brothers who shove me off the raft— once I thought I'd die down in the slime, and barely made it to shore while they hooted from the middle of the dugout.

No brothers here now. No parents.

Deep blue sky reaches up as far as it can. *This world is not my home, I'm just a-passing through,* we sing in Salem Church there on the other side of the bush, along the correction line. The church feels sleepy when you go inside on a weekday.

A plump toad takes a hop beside the grass. It was invisible, now it sits there. Six snails for another L, eight for an O. We share the snails, finish our names. *Angels beckon me from heaven's open door, I can't feel at home in this world any more...*

Letters shifting, squirming in slow motion. A breeze travels over the dugout, through the bush and out to the road. At the church it becomes a dust-devil, *Dust thou art, and to dust thou shalt return,* they said when our Grandma died, and they buried her at the back of the churchyard.

Sun standing still, names at the end of the cement, snails dropping one by one into the water again.

•

Late afternoon, autumn 1998. Salem country cemetery. I've come to visit a recently buried cousin. Ripe September sun. A poplar leaf drifts toward my father's tombstone. To the left, a fresh mound of earth is piled beside an open pit. A backhoe waits behind the carraganas—the procession will arrive soon. Passing by the new grave I look down; at the bottom, so small among scraped dirt walls, a plain gray-floral casket like my Grandmother's in 1955. Not a real petal on its lid—nor, when I look again, on the ground above. Stark hole in the prairie—the machine man hasn't had time, he'll get here, he'll get here. *And what if a badger gnaws through the coffin,* I think, *what if the corpse pushes on the lid and sits up, what if I fall on top of it?*

•

Fall 1955. In the parlour the relatives sit beside Grandma's deathbed. I look and listen through eight-year-old eyes and ears. Aunt Wanda clings tearfully to hope: *Vielleicht ist sie nicht Tod,* maybe she's not dead, maybe she's in a coma. "No, no," Grandpa's voice is resigned; and he tells how she raised her hands, asking to be lifted higher, calling loudly *Mein Heiland, mein Heiland*—Saviour, my saviour—and passed away. There is talk about whether she might have seen a vision of Christ.

Calls are made from the phone behind the kitchen door. The doctor is summoned from Rosthern, and the undertaker from Dalmeny. Grandma is declared dead. Four men roll her in a blanket, sling the ends over their shoulders, and lug her heavily toward the front porch. Halfway through the living room I hear a great gush of water from the body onto the floor—the men pause and renew their grip, and continue out to the hearse parked at the gate.

After the funeral service, Grandma's coffin is taken from the church to the cemetery. The pallbearers' ties flap in the prairie wind. A sister from Kansas hasn't arrived in time, but is expected the following day. The casket is left on the ground, tilting slightly toward the grave, to watch over itself through the night.

The next morning there are other readings and prayers. The men lower the gray box into the earth on long canvas straps, cover it with a panel, and begin shovelling. The rocks bounce on the lid, and I look hastily around at nearby headstones saying *Better in Glory than down here; Safe through the blood of Jesus; The Lord is my Shepherd Shall not want* (the I is missing). And above the remains of another eight-year-old, *Suffer the little children.*

In spring, Grandpa puts up a new monument, chiselling letters into the concrete with tools from his own workshop: *Ruhe Sanft,* rest gently.

•

Spring 1999, Saskatoon. Crossing a channel over steppingstones to a sandbar in the South Saskatchewan River. Beside the willow saplings lies a plastic grocery bag, neatly tied, plainly not left here as garbage. In the bag, a child's drawing of its family is wrapped around a cookie box; and inside the box, a white washcloth lines the cardboard, shrouding a brown hamster with folded paws—as nearly folded as they can be.

Curiosity doesn't know what to do then, after tearing open a pet's casket.

The animal must not lie here, it must be set adrift, like a little Moses on the Nile, and have words spoken over it: "You have died, but the hamster-spirit hasn't gone anywhere. And you are that." I push the box out into the current, for a moment watch it bobbing courageously in the waves, and retrace my steps home.

The next evening toward sunset I cross the channel again. Downstream, the plastic bag has washed up on the sand. Farther along, the little ark has come aground too, bent crooked from its voyage. There is no white cloth, no family picture. And the body, after its own fashion, has gone to the skies.

We are always children, obliged to walk away.

Bernadette Rule

Grandmother Fire

It wasn't the fire like they say
but the smoke that took my sight.
Grandmother, they tell me, *your eyes
are the colour of flame, your hair
twists like smoke down your back.
Crouching there all day like a bundle of sticks
you have become the fire!*

I laugh and poke into the hottest dark.
Grandmother Fire. I like that

Without me it would go out
and all the stones of all the rooms
would go cold.

My grandmother once told me
of a time when the fire went out.
It happened long ago when she was a girl.
Everyone had gone
gathering spring berries
and her grandmother fell asleep.
When the others returned the cold ash reeked
like nothing they had ever smelt before.
The old woman never did wake up.

The fire was a long time returning
    between the hands of the medicine man,
        but at last it glinted in the night eye
of a mountain lion at the edge of a spruce bough,
    then spread crackling along its length.
        The new fire blessed the old
grandmother on her way.

There's been many another fire tender since then,
    but this is the same fire.
        Its smoke took away my sight
            that you may see in the dark.

Upon the Death of a Parent

The tree had always been there.

We must have expected that it always would
offer shade and colour and background music,
a shape for the cycle of the seasons.
Then one night when a storm had passed
and the wind seemed slight, the tree fell.
Twisting to miss the house
it filled the whole yard and beyond
into the neighbours' yards.

Awakened from our sleep, we stood wondering
beside this giant, so familiar,
yet in a way so completely unknown.
Even horizontal it was taller than we were,
brilliant in its intricacies, massive in its strength.
Shyly we touched it, hands resting for a moment
on branches that had always been out of reach.

Over the next few days we arranged
to have it taken away. What else could we do?

Still, if what they say is true,
that each tree is as big or bigger underground,

we know what remains, unseen,
and reaches through the darkness yet,

on our behalf.

Ingrid Ruthig

With A View Of The Sea

This house was billed
    with a view of the sea
and with copper red door,
snowy clapboard and the dark-eyed stare
of wide windows it squatted
on the broad verdant shoulders of
restless deep blue.

Lulled by the lament of gulls
it was easy to picture a sunrise
in summer over land and out of water
in winter, its warmth to be savoured
fine mornings from bed.
You could imagine a book's page
lit by hot-sugared threads
spun through south-face panes
or the ebb of western rays
while you napped by the fire.

You clung to perfection.
So you woke, you read,
you dozed as you'd planned.

While you slept, fences sprang up
and many more houses, more trees—
saplings grew tall and broad,
taking charge of open sky
seizing all view of the sea.

Now, on unclouded dawns
when branches stretch January-bare,

if you turn to this window, just so, you can believe
      above that roof
      between these weathered-grey poles
      and so many thickened limbs

it's still there,
always impatient to be somewhere else.

Elsa Slater

The Despisèd Jug

In front of me is a medium sized jug—not crystal, but cast glass, of the type used for water or milk. In fact this is how it has been used for the last sixty years and it tells a tale and teaches a lesson.

A handsome young man (my father) and a lovely young woman (my mother) were playmates years before they matured and fell in love. Their wedding, in London, was one of those wartime affairs, which took place during my father's leave from duty in the army. Only the closest relatives attended. Family photos show my father, resplendent in his dress uniform and my mother, beautiful in a full-length lace gown. Their honeymoon was a brief holiday in Porthscatho, Cornwall and then it was back to the army for my father and home to relatives for my mother, to wait and hope that Jim, her new husband, would return safely from the war.

Unpacking the few wedding gifts they had received was like a small Christmas celebration. Giftware, as we know it, was hard to come by and many items were of plain design and practical use. My mother had an eye for pretty and artistic things and was a person of great taste. Her name was Grace and it suited her perfectly. Slim, with dark brown eyes and chestnut hair with a slight reddish tinge inherited from her mother, she was the picture of loveliness as a young, married woman. Among the various packages and parcels that she opened was a glass jug, squat in shape and rather cheap looking. My mother was not an ungrateful person but for some unknown reason she took an instant dislike to this particular item. She separated it from the other gifts and put it, along with her wedding dress, in the back of a wardrobe at her sister's home in London, where the wedding ceremony had taken place. She repacked the rest of the gifts and moved them with her to Southampton where she stayed with her parents for a few weeks.

During this time, the war was at its peak. Bombing raids occurred daily and much time was spent huddled in air raid shelters. The nightly blackout was in effect and people carefully closed heavy drapes and kept lights low. Every day that went by was a nightmare, and every dawn seemed like a miracle of survival. These were trying times especially for a newly-wedded couple, separated almost immediately after the marriage service, their few possessions stored in the homes of relatives.

Many cities suffered terrible destruction and eventually the inevitable happened—my grandparents' home in Southampton was completely destroyed. Luckily, no one was hurt or killed. The siren provided sufficient warning and my mother and her parents were safely underground when the bomb hit.

Everything was gone. The big old house that had been home to my grandparents and their five children was reduced to rubble. All they had left were the clothes they were wearing. Certainly it was the end of the wedding gifts. Counting themselves lucky to be alive, the family set about the task of rebuilding their lives as best they could. They moved to the small village of Romsey, to stay with one of my mother's sisters.

Eventually, the war ended and Jim returned home to Grace, who by now had given birth to me. Life settled down, another little girl was added to our family and the war, although not forgotten, dimmed to an unpleasant memory. Visits to relatives were always an exciting treat. The London house, where my mother's other sister lived and where my parents had held their wedding reception, had somehow survived the bombing.

On the first return visit to this house since they were married, my parents stayed in the room that my mother had occupied for a few nights immediately after her honeymoon. There in the wardrobe hung her wedding gown and there, still wrapped in cheap floral paper, was the glass jug, abandoned all those years ago. Suddenly it was transformed in her eyes from plain and ordinary to the most lovely thing in the world, the only gift to have survived. Imagine her delight as she tenderly unwrapped this memento of that happy day. Picture her remorse at having so despised it for being rather plain, her feelings on realizing that it had survived only because she disliked it. Tears flowed freely but were replaced by laughter in a whirl of sorrow, joy, shame, happiness, guilt. Finally she came to grips with the discovery that in spite of her scorn, the jug now held precious memories of her wedding day.

No article was ever wrapped as carefully and lovingly as that jug for its trip back to our home. We used it daily at the dinner table throughout my childhood to hold water, milk or flowers, and the tale of its survival was retold countless times. Various lessons in the story were underlined at every telling: "That will teach me never to despise anything." or "It's the thought that counts." and "Someone went to a lot of trouble to choose that for me."

My mother died twelve years ago and was followed by my father two years later. I returned to England to clean out the house and settle the estate. In a kitchen cupboard I found a medium sized jug—not crystal, but cast glass, of the type used for water or milk.

Russ Smith

That Small Body

—Richard Stanley Smith
9 June 1930 - 24 August 1935

I was two years old and sleeping,
while he walked out, and they
played on the sunny shore.
They thought he was napping too,
but he had gone to make his bed
off the dark side of the island.

He is a child still
who should have been my elder,
the uncertain one, first in line
for love and discipline. He persists
as a shadow in our mother's face,
and the guilt that dismays our father
when it surfaces,
like that small body.

Breaking Trail

—In memory of Barbara Lorraine Smith, 1929-2002

Sunday was snowy. You were content
for me to go alone to ski
an ungroomed trail, one that we
had broken many times together.
Powder carried on the wind
filled my tracks behind me.
I could have done with company.

That night I glazed and grilled
a trout for supper, served with rice
and green beans. You enjoyed
that meal, and television later.
Monday noon, you answered yes,
you'd have stewed prunes for lunch.
You ate them, and you thanked me.

Later, when I brought your medication
and your supper—only beans and sausages—
you were too remote to speak, to share
perplexities I couldn't understand.
Don't bother me, you seemed to say.
We never made decisions for each other,
but now I must. I called for help.

Two days later you were gone. We watched.
A monitor is the face of God.
The numbers drop toward zero
and the last flat line.
Death's bright angel, dressed
in cotton blues, removes support
till you are on your own once more.

Dying is the bitter part of death, that creeps
from toes and fingers toward the heart.

Only your fine hands by the blanket
are unchanged, hands that held
and guided, comforted and worked
for all of us, hands so relaxed we know
that now there is no tension left.

Your final day, I walked out in the snow.
Clouds that piled on the horizon
rose and shook themselves—
a few flakes only, puffs of dust.
A chickadee was whistling at a feeder.
Sparrows clambered in the cedars.
You always watched the birds.

These trifling interests that we shared
don't matter to you now. How long
before they matter much to me!—
the renovations to the house,
the carpets we agreed should be repaired,
a winter trip to Carolina, or to Portugal.
We've never been to Portugal.

Every turn reminded me, and every turn
reminds me now again, of you.
You could not sustain yourself.
We were aware of a changing wind,
of unknown drifts and obstacles.
You have stayed behind, and I
must break the trail ahead alone.

J.J. Steinfeld

I'm Waiting for You, My Dear Old Friend

Something about breaking in a new pair of running shoes, even at my advanced age, reminds me of my youth. Not that I was much of a runner when I was young. To tell the truth, I was slow and clumsy. But every spring, as if it were part of the changing of the seasons, I would get my parents to buy me a beautiful pair of running shoes—or whatever they were called in the old days—until I was old enough to save the money myself, and then I would purchase the shoes all on my own. That, as I look back, was part of my emergence into manhood: the careful selection and purchasing of my own running shoes, with my own money. And I would run, not part of any competition, not against anyone or any clock, merely run. I did build up a certain stamina and endurance, but not any speed to speak of.

As I got older, when a friend or someone would ask why I ran so much, I used to joke that I was running with God, pace for pace, and time melts away when you're in the proximity of the Supreme Being. Not that I have many friends anymore, or talk much to people, but the running is a constant in my life, from as long as I can remember. Sometimes I think I've run over the entire Island, traversed every bit of land, and whether you can see them or not, my footprints, like embedded memories, are everywhere. When I was younger, growing up in the country, I ran only in rural areas. Now, retired in the city, a widower—my precious lovely wife, gone a year, was never keen on my endless running—I run through Victoria Park, along the waterfront boardwalk, back and forth, as though there were no more sanctified terrain for running in this world, the ubiquitous crows, sentinels of the glorious park, often cawing their approval at my exertion.

My most recent pair of running shoes had the smell of my youth, even if they cost many times what running shoes cost when I was a boy. I run regardless of the weather, and a harsh wind can come off the water in winter. The worse the weather, the more of a challenge, and the more satisfaction I would take. But my running has changed. Not because of anything physical—I'll concede eight decades of earthly doings have taken a toll on my body and spirit—but because of an old man on a park bench, looking much older even than I am. I first saw this old man, his eyes as dark as a crow's and a scraggly white beard that he was forever fiddling with, two months ago, the first day of spring. Day after day he would be there. "Nice day," I would say, or "Not so nice day," or some foolish comment about the weather or the less profound aspects of life. Regardless of the weather, didn't matter if the wind was slapping furiously at your face or caressing your weary bones, he would be sitting there on the same park bench when I approached and ran past. At my apartment, I would enter the run in my log, and make a notation about the dark-eyed, scragglybearded man.

As much as I like to keep up my steady running pace, one day I slowed down, ran in place, made small talk with the man on the park bench. I started to vary the times I ran, early in the morning, before or after lunch, in the evening—he was always there. Even, on a few occasions, in the middle of the night. "What are you doing?" I asked every time. "I'm waiting for you, my dear old friend," he said without variation. The first time he told me that, I politely said that we had never met, might not yet qualify as dear old friends. Once, during a gentle Island night, I asked, "Why do you keep saying you're waiting for me?" but he did not answer, just looked skyward and pulled on his scraggly white beard as if contemplating the number of stars above us.

I changed the times I ran, pushed myself to run several times during a day, and yet he was always sitting there, waiting. I did start addressing him as my dear old friend, and I guess a friendship of sorts came to exist—an odd friendship where we did not even know each other's names or anything of our personal lives. I, to him, was simply a strange old runner and he, to me, the bearded old man on a park bench. I considered him tranquil, serene, if not a most peculiar presence in the midst of Victoria Park.

Then on one of the windiest days I could ever remember, I was startled: *he wasn't there on his park bench*. In the confusion of my thoughts about him and journeying back to my youth, my memory shimmering with all the pairs of running shoes I have run in over the Island, I found myself on the same park bench. I couldn't move, able only to raise my voice in desperation. Words turned to screams, screams to words, but none of my utterances received the slightest acknowledgement, except the occasional crow swooping down a little lower than usual before me, conveying a silent, bewildering message. I ceased my screaming, my calls for help. I looked around me, embraced the magnificence of the natural world, and I sensed, in a most difficult to explain manner, that all my life I had been running to this park bench. In my silence I could hear voices, as if the wind and crows and water and sky could make wordful sounds, and the voices were speaking softly into my aged being—*you have your place, your have your purpose, you are all of your memories*—and when certain walkers or runners pass me or stop, I say, "I'm waiting for you, my dear old friend..."

Richard Stevenson

D.I.N.K.s

It has been some years
since you squandered three
hanging around your home town
after receiving your second degree.

You had to move away (leave your kid)
to get that first plum job
Now you have your Masters, two books out,
two kids by your second wife.

You haven't seen this friend
in—What? Seven? Eight years?
After his Psych degree and several years
in dead-end jobs, a bad marriage of his own,

he's finally finished an MBA,
has met and married a bright,
attractive young nurse with her Masters
and five years' worth of equity.

They are happy happy happy
in their recently renovated older home
and explain how the mortgage payments
have been quite manageable on two salaries.

You don't doubt it as you take note
of the new stereo TV, four speakers,

dBX, equalizer, Dolby A, B, and C,
thousands of cassettes, records, and CDs.

You're perusing the Persian rug
when one of their Persian cats
glares at you with obvious disdain
for refusing to vacate its favourite chair.

You stare it down, stick out your tongue,
until the cat, bored and diffident,
slinks off like an well-fed whore
for its bowl of Tender Vittles.

Only a little twinge of envy
manages to disrupt your attention span
before drinks are poured and your gracious hosts
break out their bag of aromatic Red Hair.

You can't help but notice
the joints are thinner, if more elegant now.
Everything is thinner—even their waist lines
and especially your conversation.

Another friend drops over. He's bald,
but even richer for his pains. Is now
a senior bureaucrat in the government
you disdain. Has an ulcer and an Audi.

Conversation inevitably gets back to the music
you all listened to, and runs the gamut
from A to B of the music you listen to now.
Everyone's kudos and credentials are presented,

sniffed over like hors d'ouevres,
duly acknowledged, picked at, and put aside.
Before the night is over, you have all but
sniffed each other's privates like neutered dogs.

Your wife is disgusted at your besotted pawings.
Speeds in reverse down the long driveway
while you get down on all fours and howl at her,
and, yes, yet again, you decide to grow your hair long.

Mildred Trembley

Second Day of Mourning

—For my sister, Lillian, 1922-2001

late afternoon, the houses drawn in a cluster
to the curve of the bay like cats to a bowl
waves a light growl on the shore
the frayed daytime moon
just enough darkness behind it
to show off its pale beauty, to make it
rich as the night moon
in one stroke, swiftly, three geese flying low
everything perfectly in place, every sea-washed stone
every opened and emptied clamshell
the young seagull, resting on shore, pale brown
and the grieving woman
alone on the beach, pausing
to look, wrapped in her black winter
coat and her scarf, that woman too belongs
that woman too is held perfectly in place

Stories to Tell

In an instant, I'm back in the kitchen
watching my mother, her breasts and belly
a feather pillow tied in the middle.
She bends at the sink peeling potatoes,
moves to the wood range to stir beef stew.

On the shelf the bag of Five Roses,
the tin of Blue Ribbon and the little Dutch girl,
caught on a can, running forever.

My father's step sounds
on the back verandah. He is home for lunch,

with a head full of stories from town
to tell Mamma. The clock on the wall
has stopped at 12 o'clock noon.

Now it is twilight: I walk up the path to the house,
look in the kitchen window.
No one stands at the stove,
the table is not even set
and I remember
my mother has left, she has
wandered out to the graveyard,
found earth to lie down in.
(All those years it had waited).

My father's step on the verandah
is no longer heard.
He went looking, lay down beside her,
new stories to tell his love.

Betsy Trumpener

Blowtorch

1.

On your 24th Birthday, you and Abdi got drunk on something rough in the high-rise apartment on Lansdowne Avenue, where the trains run past your living room window. The passengers heading home late to Oakville with their briefcases looked out the GO Train window and saw you reciting Farsi poetry. Over the train's mournful whistle, they could almost read your lips: *I have searched for you in the dark graveyards...* Never mind the distance between the train's smudged windows and your verse. The commuters were as fascinated as I was. Then the train whooshed past and you stood up and vomited pickles on the carpet.

Next to me on the sofa was a small photo album with magnetic pages. That night, you showed me pictures of your dead classmates and of your *Maman-jan,* sitting alone inside a house in a village in the north of Iran.

I could see how you crossed over into Europe dressed all in white, as if you were a bride. In the photos, your arms were busy with all kinds of Bulgarian and Turkish women, girls and older ladies wearing blue eye shadow and knee-high nylons that cut into their plump calves.

2.

One night, you took off all your clothes, except your underwear, and folded them neatly on the dresser, and then you lay on your back, your good hand folded behind your head, and gazed up at the plaster swirls on the apartment ceiling, and smoked a cigarette. And time passed, but I was used to that.

And then you said *Steshenay hoshenol.* Come inside and be happy. An invitation. But your voice was almost sad, and you didn't turn to look at me. Still, I joined you. You had a hundred sweet names for me, for every part of me, even the parts that taste bitter.

That night, I dreamed the Nazis captured my father. They said they would set him free only if I pulled off my own fingers. And so I did. It was winter, and steam came from the officer's mouths as they ordered me to remove my mittens, I popped my fingers out of their sockets, one by one, and tore them from my hand. It didn't even hurt.

3.

Your elevator smelled like Texas Hash and the hookers from Newfoundland who rented the bachelor suites. It traveled slowly. I was always so eager to see you.

Not just me. Everyone was there. Abdi, who was slow and gentle and played chess in his tracksuit and his Filipino girlfriend who would whoop and giggle while they made love in the bathroom. Farid, who had glassy green eyes, which turned out later to be from heroin, and his fat wife who taught me to use glossy lipstick. And Jalal, who tried to kill himself when you were both in jail back home, who works for tips in a restaurant in a strip mall in North York and gets dizzy spells that ring in his ears.

We'd lay out a table cloth on the living room floor and eat: white rice with a crust of potato and oil, and finely diced salads with lemon and mayonnaise and chicken and pickles and cheap crystal fruit drinks from the discount grocery store below Dundas that's big as an army barracks. I'd hear rhythms and sounds and forks waving, and I felt comforted but alone.

You'd cuddle me between your legs and talk and smoke in my hair and drink chi out of a short glass and suck the sweetness from sugar cubes you clenched between your teeth. And everyone would toss down Tylenol 3s with codeine Farid always got from the doctor near Christie Pitts.

And once, Farid's fat wife put the baby to sleep in your room and then sat down for tea as if everything was fine. Then she dropped her glass and shrieked like she couldn't breathe and crawled behind the sofa screaming until the neighbor next door banged on the wall with her boots, and everyone whispered sweet words and stroked Laila's head, or what they could reach of it, until she came out of hiding.

4.

You were the tough one. The flat nose, the sharp bones, the firm, scarred hands. Hands that made me want to kiss you. You would come in at four in the morning from delivering pizza, after a troop of kids from Jane and Finch had bashed a bruise across the back of your head with a bike chain, trying to get your cash, or an old man in slippers had drawn out his penis in the elevator, while your hands were full of pizza. I would wake up with you on top of me, and a flat box of Hawaiian Deluxe in the fridge, the cheese turning hard in the cold.

You were so goddamn beautiful I let you wake me up and tie me to the curtains and do me like that, with the moon beating down outside on the empty train tracks.

5.

The night I woke up smelling rancid aftershave, a bitter lemon stink, it was you. Your kidneys, turning on their stem. As if long ago, they'd been struck hard enough and long enough to keep them spinning, now, years later.

I had never heard you scream.

I sped you down Dundas Street although I couldn't drive, steering between the shine of streetlights on the streetcar tracks.

The lights in Emergency were blinding and you barely knew me. One nurse was annoyed by your name and jammed a thermometer up your ass. She asked you where it hurt in a booming voice, her lips moving like a giant puppet's mouth, as if you were deaf, and the doctor yanked on your penis with metal tongs, as if that would make it better.

You've told me many things, but never this.

You tell me your first lover's breasts were perfect tight plums under your hands in her hot room. That you used to leave with your school friends before light to hike in the mountains, and stop to eat a goat head along the way. That you played accordion in a wedding band, even though you were too young. That you and Jalal used to lie down together on a bunk bed in the Mashad barracks and he'd read poetry into your hair:

A mountain begins with the first
rock and man with the first pain...

That you shot at enemy planes flying over the swampy islands of Majnoon, but the real battle was keeping the rats off your pillow at night. That coming out of jail, you and Jalal took turns with an addict no older than yourselves, who laid her hijab and raincoat carefully across a chair before lying down on the floor.

"What a short, sad night," you said.

You even told me how you planned to die, after you thought you'd changed your mind. How you planned to turn on the gas oven in the apartment on Lansdowne, the oven in which you cooked pans of chicken kebob and kept the rice warm. The stove on which we made chi, which you drank from a glass with a sugar cube gritted between your teeth. How I'd ride up in the slow elevator and open the door and see your empty tea glass on the counter.

You told me many things.

7.

But never this.

What happened in a room in the basement of the Mashad military jail.

That they opened your back with a cable as thick as your throat. That they turned your kidneys on their stem trying to reach your voice box. That they shrouded your curls in a hood and beat at you until you looked like someone else.

I thought you told me everything. You even told me how you planned to kill yourself. How you'd turn on the gas, and later, how I'd open the door and say, "Honey, I'm home."

8.

There was always chicken kebob cooking in the oven and a pot of rice on the stove in the apartment on Lansdowne, and I'd take the elevator up, and it was slow, but I didn't mind.

Everyone would be there, and they'd be drinking tea, and cooking opium on the coffee table with a blowtorch, and filling the air with hot sweet smoke, and poetry, and someone would stand up and declare:

It's night

Air standing like a hot swollen body…

And tonight the neighbor's pallid kids are trying to crawl across the balcony divide in the summer heat, and the neighbor knocks on the door and says she's Brenda and she wants to come in.

And Brenda sits on the floor with a plate of kebob and offers to read your palm. And I watch as you grant her your firm, scarred hand. And she holds it and traces the scars. And you stare at her as if she has something you need, and you ask her how it will all turn out.

Liz Urainetz

Ashes

Autumn here and a cold wind wends around the faltering heat. My bike rolls down Christie in the morning, watching the parks and the sky and the trees, the cold scorches my face and hands, dips down my collar to my chest, legs pumping into the easy action of the glide. I am alive. I can move. The asphalt moves under me without complaint, white curb and sidewalk following, parked cars narrow the road to squish and caution. My stomach tightens into the pump of my legs, my spine stretched to arc, arms straight, wrists propping the weight of me onto cold metal. The world is yellow and cold. Familiar slopes and bumps and curves, traffic lights at Bloor and College, churches and stores, bakeries and vegetable marts. I've walked here so often scrunched in terror, dissociating into light and glass; walked these blocks in heat and rain and night, broken open from the gut. Here I glide.

Then he was with me, the action of his violence blotting the streets from my mind, breaking every corner of thought into schism; every rumbling car was headed straight at me. I had to be quick when my heart was heavy, could not think of tomorrow's dinner or next week's movie. Quick and sharp. He lived with me this way, in violence, as memory, for years. Now he is gone and the cars really do pass by, as my life has passed by, warm, breathy, encased in steel and glass, my fingers fiddling the buttons under the dash for a song, some news, a conversation between strangers who have strong opinions about war, marigolds, taxes, and dog poo. Strong enough to call. From Moncton, Salt Spring, Lafayette, Muenster. Though, it's true, the call is free, the words are free, and listening only costs time and the energy of a radio button. We used to have knobs, things we could turn, a flow of adjustment to preference. Now it is preprogrammed and I push, for volume, for sound, for interest, radio waves jumping frequency to frequency; they jump where they want, land half-station, off-station, and I'm left with Neil Diamond again, strong voice, pop craft, and a good tune for all that.

Violence lives in the blood, right beside desire. Close, too close, they intertwine, get mixed up, a tangle of fine chains lumped in my bones so I can not tell the difference. When Sam said he loved me I couldn't tell if he wanted to hit me or make love. We sat all night on the edge of our couches, corner to corner, quiet lights glowing beside our shoulders, our legs wrapped under each of our bodies, separate where they could have been clasped. How much would it take to walk across a room–this room, this walk. For me it felt like centuries. Decades away from the first blow but I still feel it in my belly, across my legs, hitting the floor with such a thud, such a scream, I thought we were in the movies, and maybe I slipped there, into celluloid and dream, and the story of someone else's life trimmed and shortened into highlights, with meaningful pauses standing for years and depth. Maybe I slipped there, and slipped again, with the baby, the motel, the summer I kept five lovers, one for every block, one for every blow, for every self I've managed to resurrect from the rubble, not ashes, of what I had resurrected before. No one knows where the wild goose goes. Not even the goose.

Centuries, then, decades. This small walk, us on the edge, and the slip into the warmth I know so well, of another body wanting me back, hands alive around my heart and every lover becomes particular in the similarity of desire, bliss, in the desperate need of his particular eyes, his hair, his mind talking words in a language I know so well but do not, do not understand. Ah bliss. Oh desire. Oh my lover. Take my heart into your breathless soul, take me in as a woman takes a lover in, into the body not whole but deep, held, clutched with the contractions of release.

There's the blow.

The hand coming out of nowhere to slap the back of the head, the belt whipping the blood to heat. Yes. I know it well. This heat. This action. The heart thumping wild into dizzy breath. The intrusion of love into the soul. I know it well, how to take a man in, make him feel at home. I can become his mother, his sister, his child. Listen well and touch softly, become hard as hard becomes his need.

We spoke all night, all day, all night. And I wanted to take him home, wanted him to become me, to become this desperation, this despair. But rescued him at the last minute, every minute, to the last. The ocean was there, down the road, at the docks. And the yachts moored. And the ferries howling caution to the shore.

Oh but I wanted him badly. Wanted to slip, to fall, to slip him into me like a penny, earned, saved, kept; jangling around memory like a lost something that won't give up.

There he sits, gentle as a lamb, on the other side of the room while I sit in this chair, the chair I sat in then, babbling broken weeping. He is across the room and I am full of desire; and full, too, with the need of lambs.

Emmanuelle Vivier

So heavy inside

I used to roam the earth
feet barely touching
the ground

until the day you died

suddenly I knew
the closeness of death
a sadness so immense
it pulled me to you

when you see
the ones you love
for the last time
and go on living
with only the memories
that lie beneath
the surface of the earth
each death so heavy
inside

dragging you further down
some days it feels
as though you are sinking
thigh-deep into the soil
the ground caving in
beneath you

Naomi Beth Wakan

Telling My Brain

I am telling my brain
I have lost a breast.
I draw a diagram for it
And go over it time and
Time again, but my brain
Is reluctant to know.
"Not two curves, but
One curve" I say firmly,
But my brain still sends pain
To the air above my chest.
"Don't be foolish," I implore,
"Use your brains," I cry inanely,
And it is only after I have told
It one thousand and one times,
That a total blank appears where
There was a once a mound.
It is only then that I realize
That it's time to tell
myself.

Betty Warrington-Kearsley

All That's Skin Deep

When I was small and fell
and grazed my knee
my Chinese grandmother would lift me high
and reciting comfort me:
tuk jik, tuk chuk
mi puere, bo mi kuq
her ancient mantra inevitably
removing all disaster from me,

a spell, when I was old enough to know
meant well:
all that is skin-deep that doesn't ravage bone
always heals however slow;
it does not damage
or destroy the force of life within
but deploys without reserve
all means to preserve dear life and limb.

When I awoke and heard the surgeon say:
'I think I've got it all, every bit of it,
the cancer's gone,
move on now and live
in fullness of your being
the extended life that might not have been,'
I rejoiced and felt my grandma's childhood ditty
pulse beneath those breasts I lost that saved me.

Jessica Warsh

Packrat's Lament

you said I have a remarkable memory
but I have forgotten you now

the scent of your skin is no bottled breeze
I can unseal and sniff in my dreams

you are not scent, but absent

at night
without my beckoning
other worlds appear
preceding you
the taste of your lips unknown

I wake to the glint of frozen decades
their wax fruit still bouncing off sun

perhaps I did not know you enough to wax-trap
a trace of your smile
prepare for exhibit the bungle of relics
movie stubs, bills,
what the rubbish pile coughed

it did not wheeze you into marquee lights for the evening show
though I would have liked to keep your face at hand
if only for entertainment

but hands have a way of reaching back
and poking about in the dark

combing the beach for prized shells
and blindly picking up drift
combing my hair
for pockets of your scent

since that first day
I could smell it
on my pillow

Bereavement

Evening pressing down so hard
is a dark child
turning his feet in the sky,
a wombling from east to west belly,
       curling his leg round the day:

the infant turning presses his heels
into uncharted parts of the galaxy.

It is not clear at first that this new pain
(shooting through the new points of light)
is anything but nightfall
       dropping harder, blacker than before.

But, like pain, the child will be borne
and loss will be a new coupling:
       the fusion of you
       with genes of your memory
       the intercourse of widow and wife.

Yes, now it is evening, Explorer,
and morning sickness splashes out stars
       they pierce
       far
       into the deep:
you discover them in leaving things behind.

but slowly: onward

working the keen, a lone skiff on the birth waves,
       traveling by memory,
       which is no map at all,

Sees
       the child stand on his own,
       step out the face of the lake
       (the face whose absence let in the flood)

She sees back
in the gestures of new sky.

Suppertime

Perhaps I have not left room for you, Spring, I think
as March becomes April.
How becoming is the sun on your streets, my city;
the slow gas simmer from east to west
releases cooking odours
from the dead ground.

Rain is onions frying:
it makes us hungry
for what is coming as sure as suppertime.

We, who have not eaten since the last harvest apples
We, anorexic smokers of chimneys and hash
Drinkers of sour mash from the autumn woods' floor:
We are smelling onions
            and surprised—

I saw in the dazed
faces of street walkers the unbelieving gaze
at 10 degree weather,
the end of the necessity
to button heavy coats—

I saw that no one had left room.

After the glut of snow, the feast
of sleepers on smoke and sour mash
and an absence of light,

we are all full of ashes,
which have been used since Prometheus
as a condiment.

Sylvia M. Warsh

Krakow by Night

She travels back to Poland every night,
wafts through the ghetto square
like the perfume of schmalz herring and
yeasty challah that has been absent
these fifty years
like her.
The earth-bred babushkas arrange
turnips in their stalls beneath
the empty vaulted sky
do not see her, feel her, miss her
as she floats down the inevitable lanes
of *Kazimierz* searching
for the shape of her mother
reclining in the sweet little courtyard,
the gentle arc of her mother
that she yearns to clasp but
which refuses her dream
like the shouts on stone of Jewish children playing,
replaced by silence,
a keen edge of silence that
tears open her heart each night
when she travels back to Poland.

Love Song to the Food Chain

There is something sinister about
the buzzing of flies,
the collective memory of besieged flesh
in the night of soil,
the sound our genes pass on
of maggots and flies singing
their own love songs

to the food chain, our co-opted bodies
sweetening the trip for
fungus and lilies that rise
in the wake of shredded marrow bone,
muscle, heart fused to earth in
an embrace so round
there is no beginning,
no end,
a circle of sound
we hear in our
deepest sleep.

If you think Roses love you

You are a fool if you plant roses,
those loose-lipped dripping honey lovelies
whose petal mouths drink your energy,
your work as if you owed them,
as if you too could throw back the sun
and merely exhale perfume to please.

You are a fool if you think roses love you.
Their indifferent thorns catch skin
at its most vulnerable
when it's stretched to curl around stems
seeking love.
They are not interested in you
but gaze at the worker bees
loose in the sky.
The spider, the earwig that find their lavish creases
they embrace, but not you,
the caretaker of their life,
the one who mounds the soil in November
to bury their waning crown,
the one who weeps over
the ribs of spent crimson velvet
and watches and waits and
hates the passing months till spring.

Zacariah Wells

The Doctor, Over Supper, Recalls a Quirk in the Medical History of Baffin Island

—*For Paul Stubbing*

Ten, fifteen years ago
we got a lot of gunshot guts
in men from Cape Dorset—

I bet half the men there have the scars today.

Word got around, see
that shooting yourself with a .22
isn't likely to do
much damage.

We averaged round a case a week.
I got so sick of it once I drew a slow X
over the heart of one man
with my finger,
told him to aim there
next time.

Yep, the men shot themselves for airfare
& the women got knocked up
to go South for abortions—

the men were faking the end of life;
the women, the beginnings.

Except this one girl broke the pattern,
used a gun instead of a prick

Got her free trip alright—
didn't ever walk again.

A lot less bullet wounds
out of Dorset after that.

Still the odd abortion, though—

Joanna Weston

A Garden for Mother

serene among daffodils
Mother arranged tulips in pewter

hung sunflowers from rafters
where moonlight stroked them
grey and silver
in her garden of searchlights

she dug holes to plant pilots
as they fell from the sky
to flower as violets

paint touched her canvas
into misted apple blossom
before she died
in a magic broadcast by waves
        of elderflower, lilac and peony
before summer could merge every season
        in a cup of fermented petals

For Harold, Who Drowned Age 14

Ten years since he played a banjo,
plucked notes from fir trees
and dropped them in the river.

I saw his music carried on small waves
down under the bank where he used
to sail hazelnuts to the ocean.

Today each half-tone rises
and is cried back to the beach
where I stand watching

as that elfin boy rides in the sea
with a sail of blown foam
and oars made of kelp

to play among the white-caps
where angels mend their harps
and waves break over my hands.

Notes on the Contributors

Kelley Aitken is the author of the short story collection: *Love in Warm Climate* (The Porcupine's Quill, 1998). She currently lives in Toronto with her partner. **Segun Akinlolu** has published two volumes of textual poetry and a poetry CD. Read more about him and his work at www.beautifulnubia.com. **Shari Andrews** lives in New Maryland, New Brunswick. Her most recent book is *Bones about to Bloom* (Oberon Press, 2001). **Jacqueline Bell's** work has appeared most recently in Vue magazine as the winning entry for the Vocal Locals contest for LitFest 2003. **Roger Bell** lives in Ontario. His forthcoming book is *The Pissing Women of Lafontaine*. His last book was *When The Devil Calls* (Black Moss Press, 2000). **Marianne Bluger** has written eight collections of poetry the latest being *Early Morning Pieces* (Buschek Books, spring 2004). **Nollaig Bonar,** born in Dublin, now lives in Charlottetown, P.E.I., where she is an Occupational Therapist by day and a poet by night. **Virginia Boudreau** lives in the lovely seaside community of Yarmouth, Nova Scotia with her family. She works as an early literacy teacher. **Laurie Brinklow** is a writer and editor, and publisher of Island Studies and Acorn Press. She won the Writers' Federation of Nova Scotia Poetry Prize in 1998, and has had poems published in various journals and anthologies. Ottawa writer **Ronnie R. Brown** is the author of three books of poetry. Her most recent, *Photographic Evidence* (Black Moss, 2000), was short-listed for the Archibald Lampman Award. **Margo Button** has published three poetry books, the most recent being *The Elders' Palace* (Oolichan, 2002). She lives in Victoria, B.C. and New Zealand. **Lauren Carter** has had poetry published in *Grain, Event, Prairie Fire* and other literary journals. She lives with her husband in central Ontario. *Untying the tongue* (Black Moss, 2002) is **Gregory M. Cook's** latest book of poems. *One Heart, One Way Alden Nowlan: a writer's life* (Pottersfield Press, 2003) is his biography of long-time friend Alden Nowlan (1933-1983). **Carlinda D'Alimonte** is a poet and high school English and creative writing teacher who published her first book of poetry, *Now That We Know Who We Are* in 2004 by Black Moss Press. She lives in Tecumseh, Ontario. **Julie Dennison** teaches English at the University of Prince Edward Island. Her most recent publication is a chapbook entitled *The Medium.* **Yvette Doucette** is an Islander who has been writing poetry since she was seven. She has dabbled in acting and is currently creating a monologue as part of an eight-woman show,

Solo Works. **Jannie Edwards** lives and writes in Edmonton where she teaches at Grant MacEwan College. Her first book of poetry is *The Possibilities of Thirst.* **Mark Featherstone** is a biologist at McGill University and lives in Montreal West. His work has appeared in *Arc, HMS Beagle* and *Mandrake Poetry Review.* Born in northern England, **Pam Galloway** now lives in Vancouver. Her writing often explores themes of loss and belonging common to the immigrant experience. **Kathleen Hamilton** is a writer who lives and writes in Montague P.E.I. **gillian harding-russell's** first poetry collection, *Candles in my Head* (Ekstasis Editions) came out in 2001. **Steven Heighton's** first poetry book, *Stalin's Carnival* (Quarry Press), won the Lampert Award in 1990, and his second, *The Ecstasy of Skeptics* (The House of Anansi), was a '95 Governor General's Award finalist. The poems appearing in this anthology are from *The Address Book,* published by Anansi in spring 2004. **David Helwig** lived most of his life in Ontario, but moved to P.E.I. in 1996. He is the author of many books, poetry, fiction and essays. A book-length poem, *The Year One,* was published by Gaspereau in spring of 2004 and won theWFNS Atlantic Poetry Prize for 2005. **LA Henry** teaches English literature at St. Stephen's University in St. Stephen, N.B. Along with teaching and writing, she plays bass guitar both in church worship groups and in several local pop/rock bands. **Eileen Holland** lives with her family in Coquitlam, B.C. where she teaches elementary school. She has had a number of articles and personal essays published. She hopes to hear of a cure for Lou Gehrig's Disease someday soon. **Cornelia Hoogland** is a poet, playwright and scholar. Hoogland's latest book *Cuba Journal: Language and Writing* (Black Moss Press, 2003) has toured Cuba and the Philippines. Hoogland lives in London, Ontario. **Gary Hyland** is a Moose Jaw writer whose most recent book of poetry is *The Work of Snow* (Thistledown) the 2003 winner of the John V. Hicks Memorial Poetry Manuscript Award. **Beth E. Janzen** wrote the first draft of "Letter to Corinth" while travelling in Greece with her husband in 1998. Her poetry chapbook, *Night Vanishes,* was published in 2004. She lives in Charlottetown, P.E.I.. **Joanne Jefferson** is a poet, performer, and freelance writer who studied theatre and literature at Acadia and Dalhousie and now lives in West LaHave, Nova Scotia. **Gail Johnston** divides her time between the two worlds which provide the impetus for her writing: Lasqueti Island and Vancouver, B.C. **Deirdre Kessler** is author of a dozen books for young readers, including award-winning *Brupp Rides Again* and *Lobster in My Pocket* (Ragweed Press). She teaches creative writing at the University of Prince Edward Island. **Norman G. Kester,** the South African-born editor of ground-breaking *Liberating Minds* (McFarland and Company) recently participated in Poetry Africa 2003 in his native South Africa and placed a tombstone on his mother's unmarked grave to give her a final home. **John B. Lee,** recently named poet laureate of Brantford, Ont., has a new book with Black Moss *Poems for The Pornographer's Daughter* coming out this year. **Malca Litovitz's** second poetry collection, *At the Moonbean Café,* is now available from Guernica Editions. She teaches at Seneca College in Toronto. **Hugh MacDonald's** fourth poetry collection is *Cold Against the Heart* (Black Moss Press). He has a childrens' book called *Chung Lee Loves Lobsters* (Annick Press) and several edited books. He was the 2004 recipient of the Award for Distinguished Contribution to the Literary Arts on Prince Edward Island. **Steve McCabe** is a poet and multidisciplinary visual artist. Originally from the American midwest he now lives in Toronto. He is the author of two books of poetry. **Robin McGrath's** most recent adult novel, *Donovan's Station* (Killick Press), was on the Canada-Caribbean Shortlist for The Commonwealth Prize. She lives in Beachy Cove, Newfoundland. **rob mclennan** is an Ottawa-based poet, has published nine collections of poetry. He is editor of, among others, *Groundswell: best of above/ground press.* **Christina McRae** is a freelance writer and editor specializing in scientific/technical communications. She was awarded first place in the 2001 Atlantic Writing Competition for poetry. **Dianne Hicks Morrow** is award-winning P.E.I. poet whose first collection is *Long Reach Home* (The Acorn Press). **Kit Pepper** has lived on Gabriola Island, B.C. for eleven years where she's raised three sons. She works part-time at Malaspina University-College in Nanaimo and has been published in a number of Canadian literary journals. **Marilyn Gear Pilling** of Hamilton, where she teaches at McMaster University, published *The Field Next To Love* with Black Moss Press in 2002. When **Barbara Rager** retired from 30 years of teaching high school writing, she found a job as a guidance counsellor at an Islamic school in Ottawa, where she lives with her husband of thirty-two years, whom she married on a beach on Panmure Island, P.E.I. **Lloyd Ratzlaff** is a former minister, counsellor, and university lecturer who writes from Saskatoon. He is the author of *The Crow Who Tampered With Time* (Thistledown Press). **Bernadette Rule** has had five collections of poetry published, most recently *The Weight Of Flames* (Saint Thomas Poetry Series, Toronto). She teaches in the Writing at McMaster Univesity and chairs the Hamilton Poetry Centre. **Ingrid Ruthig,** who lives neaer Toronto, is an architect by profession and now writes full-time, and is currently completing her first collection of poetry, *Water From the Moon*. **Elsa Slater** draws heavily upon her English upbringing for her poetry and stories. She lives in Ottawa, where she is also an enthusiastic flute player. Ottawa writer **E. Russell Smith's** poetry has appeared in litmags across Canada as well as in Britain and India. His most recent collection is *Why We Stand Facing South* (Moonstone). **J. J. Steinfeld** lives in Charlottetown, has published a novel and nine short story collections and was the 2003 recipient of the Award for Distinguished Contribution to the Literary Arts on Prince Edward Island. **Richard Stevenson** of Lethbridge, Alberta, teaches English and Creative Writing courses at the community college there. He is the author of fifteen published collections. **Mildred Tremblay** lives in Nanaimo. A book of her poetry, *Old Woman Comes Out of Her Cave,* was published by Oolichan Books in 2001. **Betsy Trumpener** lives in northern B.C. where she works as a journalist. Her fiction has been anthologized and broadcast on CBC Radio. **Elizabeth Ukrainetz** is a Toronto writer working on her second novel. **Emanuelle Vivier,** originally from Paris, France, is a poet and translator living in Windsor, Ont. **Naomi Beth Wakan** has written/compiled over thirty books. Her writing has appeared in many magazines including *Geist* and *Room of One's Own*. **Betty P. Warrington-Kearsley** is of English and Chinese parentage. She writes short stories and poetry, some of which have been published in Canada, England and the U.S.A, and several have won prizes. **Jessica Warsh's** work has previously appeared in *Acta Victoriana* and the *UC Review*. **Sylvia Maultash Warsh's** second novel, *Find Me Again,* was published by Dundurn Press in November, 2003. Her stories and poetry have appeared in magazines. She also teaches writing to seniors. **Zachariah Wells,** originally from PEI, has lived in Ottawa, Montreal, Iqaluit, Resolute Bay, and now in Halifax. He has worked as an ice-cream slinger, bartender, actor, security guard, airline cargo handler and agent. **Joanna M. Weston** is a full-time writer of poetry, short-stories and reviews and has had work published internationally in journals and anthologies.